WYLAND
THE WHALING WALLS

WYLAND
THE WHALING WALLS

INTRODUCTION by Dr. Roger Payne
TEXT by Mark Doyle
WORDS by WYLAND

A SERIES OF 100 LIFESIZE MURALS BY WYLAND DEDICATED TO SAVING OUR OCEANS

Wyland The Whaling Walls
Copyright © 1997 Wyland Studios, LLC

Artwork © 1995 Wyland
All quotes by Wyland © 1995 Wyland

All rights Reserved

No part of this book may be reproduced or transmitted in any form by any means, electronic or mechanical, including photocopying and recording, or by any information storage or retrieval system, without written permission from the copyright holders, except for brief passages quoted by a reviewer in a newspaper or magazine.

First published in U.S.A. by Wyland Studios, LLC
2171 Laguna Canyon Road, Laguna Beach, California U.S.A. 92651

Library of Congress Catalog Card Number 94-060365

First Edition 1995

U.S.A. Cataloging in Publication Data

Wyland, 1956
Wyland The Whaling Walls

ISBN 1-884840-10-8

Cover Photo by:
Denise Marie Luko

Produced by:
Wyland Studios, LLC
2171 Laguna Canyon Road, Laguna Beach, California U.S.A. 92651

The publisher would like to thank the following people whose support and encouragement made this book a dream come true.
Jacques Cousteau, Angela Eaton, Mark Doyle, Jennifer Mueller, Lisa Thornton, Dan Fogelberg, Jimmy Buffett, Ted Danson, Darlene Wyland, Robert Wyland, Steve Wyland, Bill Wyland, Tom Wyland, Tom Klingenmeier, Dick Lyday, Roy Chavez, Bob Eggert, Brian Spencer, Julie Edwards and Team Wyland.

The spirit of the Whaling Walls is dedicated to Pam Lagerbauer who gave so much of herself to me and my crew, we love you Pam.

Also, I need to thank all my friends and collectors throughout the world for continuing to support me and believing in my vision.

I would also like to thank all the people around the world who have worked to protect our ocean friends, this book is dedicated to you.

It is my hope that this book in some small way may make a difference.

NOTICE

This book may not be reproduced in any manner or the pages or artwork applied to any materials listed but not limited to the following:

-Cut, trimmed or sized to alter the existing trim size of the pages.
-Laminated, transferred or applied to any substance, form or surface.
-Carved, molded or formed in any manner in any material.
-Lifted or removed chemically or by any other means, or transferred to produce slides or transparencies.
-Used as promotional aids, premiums, advertising, for non-profit, or educational purposes.
-Engraved, embossed, etched or copied by any means onto any surfaces whether metallic, foil, transparent or translucent.
-Matted or framed with the intent to create other products for sale or resale or profit in any manner whatsoever, without express written consent from:

Wyland Studios, LLC
2171 Laguna Canyon Road, Laguna Beach, California U.S.A. 92651
Visit our Internet web site at http://**www.wyland.com**

Artist painting life-size humpback whale - Wilmington, DE 1993
▶

This book is dedicated to Jacques-Yves Cousteau

▲ photo © The Cousteau Society

painting on skyclimber scaffolding
7 stories above the ground,
Norfolk, VA 1993
▶

6

...If whales could see life-size portraits of themselves painted on sea walls, what would they think?...

Detail, painting right whale fluke

▲ Directing scaffolding crew, Whaling Wall 50, Atlanta, GA 1993

...One person can indeed make a difference...

▲ Artist with spray gun

CONTENTS

INTRODUCTION by Dr. Roger Payne
WORDS by WYLAND

I.   EARLY INFLUENCES - BY MARK DOYLE/15

II.   THE ART OF SAVING WHALES/27

III.   THE FIRST WHALING WALL/35

IV.   WHALING WALLS/45

V.   PAINTING THE LARGEST MURAL IN THE WORLD/93

VI.   17 MURALS, 17 CITIES, 17 WEEKS/99

VII. PAINTING GIANT MURALS/143

VIII. DIVING WITH WHALES/153

IX.   ORIGINAL PAINTINGS/161

X.   SCULPTURE/177

XI.   CHILDREN'S GALLERY/185

XII. VISION/191

      WHALING WALL LOCATIONS/196

▲ Home studio, North Shore of Oahu, Hawaii

Wyland

INTRODUCTION
Dr. Roger Payne

"In my mind's eye, I see whales out there large and small, all spyhopping and craning their necks, trying to get glimpses of Wyland's work"

This book is about someone with a unique talent - a kind of pied piper who travels through the world leaving murals in his wake, a kind of Johnny Appleseed with a paint brush. Wyland did his first Whaling Wall in 1981 in Laguna Beach, California. It was 140 feet long and twenty-six feet high. Since then he has done 53 more. The speed with which he paints his murals is as dazzling as the final result. On the last day there is always a ceremony and someone - a mayor, an actor, a sports figure, a C.E.O., an educator, a statesman, or a conservationist - gets to dedicate the wall. Several friends of mine have dedicated Wyland walls; I've even had the honor myself. It was on August 8th in 1993 - and the wall was one of the two smallest Wyland has done (singer/songwriter, Jimmy Buffet got to do the other). It's at the National Zoo in Washington, D.C. - a perfect little gem. Wyland even used a flaw in the concrete to create a shadow in the pupil of the painting (harbor porpoises are the smallest of the toothed whales).

The dedication ceremony came on a lovely, warm afternoon, and as I sat listening to the other speakers trying to explain just why it is that they feel so warmly about what Wyland accomplishes, I had the chance to reflect on what a truly unique fellow he is.

Wyland is a true original, a delightful, true original. Having spent much of my life trying to instill whales more firmly into human culture, my hat is off to this guy. To get an idea of just what it is that he accomplishes each time he paints a wall, it may help to imagine the process: Imagine first, the months of negotiations regarding some wall he is about to paint. And, when the project is finally agreed, imagine going up to that wall - sometimes on a building so ugly it was abandoned by the architects who conceived it before they even saw it built, and has been the despair of its owners ever since. And imagine assembling the paints, and rigging the staging, and roping off the area below (and finding parking for the truck with all the gear, and food for all your helpers). And imagine climbing onto the staging and as it lifts you up across what is sometimes several acres of blank wall, loading the paint into your spray gun, starting the compressor, and then, while leaning back as far as you can (so as to have as much of an overview as possible - really out of the question, given that you are pressed right against the wall) deciding what the design will be. (Wyland never knows what he is going to paint until he is on site with his spray gun in hand). And as you start to paint, imagine dealing with windstorms, and rainstorms, and lightning, and blisteringly hot days, and have to come down to use the bathroom or to eat (he uses a cellular phone so he can talk with people while he paints. I have talked with him at such times, the sounds of traffic far below seeming like some far away dream.) And imagine fielding the questions of the curious every time you come down off your scaffold, and the pressure on you each time you think about the fact that someone is arranging for the press to be present just six days from now and that by then the wall must be finished, and ready for the dedication ceremony. Yet one of the most delightful things about Wyland is that during all this madness and pressure he seems to be the person having the most fun.

And then there is that other most interesting and most unexpected aspect of Wyland's work: he doesn't charge for painting a wall. How does he do it you ask? Did he inherit a fortune? None. He gets the paints, the staging and a truck contributed. That's part of the project.

In 1993 Wyland painted seventeen walls in seventeen east coast tour cities in seventeen weeks. A year before that he painted the world's largest mural (three and a third vertical acres) in Long Beach, California, and in 1987 and again in 1989 he painted murals on walls in Japan. He made the seventeen city tour along the east coast of the United States because most of his other U.S. walls were on the west coast and he wanted to see whales on east coast walls. Considering that many of the walls Wyland has painted were eyesores before he turned them into murals, he is obviously someone with the ability to frustrate any architect - and that can't be all bad considering the standard of much of today's municipal architecture. (I can think of several buildings I wish he had painted). He turned the side of an ugly power generation station into a spectacular scene and a convention center that looked like a gas storage tank into the world's largest mural - a circular mural at that. Progress, true progress.

Why is it that when the painter of the world's largest murals was born, that it should have been whales he painted? It's just one more example of the things that whales inspire in us. It is not just their size. If it were, there would have been Wylands long ago painting murals of elephants and brontosauruses on buildings. No, this charming madness had to emerge with whales. They seem to be the animals that capture our imagination more than others do.

I salute you Wyland and I suspect that whales salute you too. In my mind's eye, I see whales out there large and small, all spyhopping and craning their necks, trying to get glimpses of your work.

I like to think that if global warming ever melts the ice caps, and the oceans flood our coastal cities, that the first things the whales will visit in their new domain will be the Wyland murals.

Dr. Roger Payne
Whale Biologist

EARLY INFLUENCES
A Profile by Mark Doyle

...In France I would be an *artiste*,
but in America I'm just another painter...

▲ Artist at Dali museum, Spain 1989

16

▲ Artist at two years

I
EARLY INFLUENCES

I was born under a water sign — Cancer, the Crab. I don't know exactly why I had this attraction to the water, but I did and was drawn to it very early. Being born in Michigan, I was surrounded by lakes, including the Great Lakes. My family spent a lot of time visiting my Aunt Barbara and my Uncle Bob, who lived on Cass Lake. But I was not able to enter the water for years because of my disability — I was born with a club foot. Since the day I was born, the very first day, I was put into a cast to correct my leg. I went through 11 surgeries by the time I was seven years old.

I still remember being out at Aunt Barbara's place, right on the lake. To me, as a small kid, this was the ocean — my own little ocean. It was hard for me to watch my brothers, my cousins and all my friends go running out into the lake and enjoying the water, while I had to stay on the bank. But I found that the time I spent on shore gave me the opportunity to develop my other passion — art. Art and water became the two major forces in my life, just as they are today.

I started drawing and painting when I was three. At the time, dinosaurs were the big subject for me, and they still are. The dinosaurs of yesterday are the whales of today. They now live beneath our oceans. I'm constantly aware that the whales may very well go the way of the dinosaurs if man continues on the path of destroying the environment at the rate at which it is now happening.

Eventually, the cast on my foot came off. The first time I ran into the water I felt like I had been reborn, like I belonged there. Even now, I'm more comfortable in the water than out. Today, I have to be in the water in some form at least once a day or I don't feel right. The fact is that all life started in the ocean — in the water. So it's all coming full circle, and I feel real connected to that. The ocean continues to be the primary force in my life, and the inspiration for my life's work.

As I grew older, my dad would take us to Lake Michigan. Anyone who has experienced this large body of water knows it has waves. We would spend all day bodysurfing the waves and enjoying ourselves. Later, as I began to understand geography, I realized it wasn't the real ocean. But it was the next best thing. I always wondered why I wasn't born near the ocean because I had such a longing for it. I had the feeling I'd been there before, and I wanted to somehow make my way west to the Pacific.

Growing up in Detroit, I always felt I was caught in a transitional period. When I had learned everything I could, I would wrap everything up and work my way out to the West Coast. I thought about it daily. In fact, I think the way I finally got to the ocean was by painting it. Most of my work at the time revolved around the ocean. I painted figures and still-life and the other things most artists are trained for in their early years, but in my spare time I painted the sea.

A very early influence was my first-grade art teacher. She saw that I spent a lot of time drawing and sketching in class and sat down with me and spent a good portion of the day teaching me how to draw faces and figures. She spent some quality time with me and told me that if I wanted, I could be a very fine artist. This made a tremendous impression on me, so much so that I try to share my knowledge and inspire some of the younger children I encounter. If I could be so impacted by one teacher taking a little time with me, then maybe I can have an even greater impact on young artists of today. To spend some time with the children who are watching me paint these giant murals, and try to encourage them in their studies and art. That's one of the most important contributions I can make as an artist.

Without a doubt, art class was my favorite class all the way through school. I always found myself trying to dodge as many other classes as I could and get back to my art. For the most part, the art teachers liked me and understood. In the fourth grade, my art teacher was so taken with the art another student and I were doing that she let us design our own cartoon — a column cartoon for our little school newspaper. It was a Western of all things. It was neat because we illustrated it, developed the characters and wrote it. The students would always look for the latest cartoon, and being considered promising young artists gained us a lot of attention and even some fringe benefits, all of which was very encouraging.

When I got to the seventh grade, I bonded closely with Mrs. Stevens, who encouraged me even more during the three years I attended her classes. She recognized that I was emerging as the "school artist" and tried to be very supportive. I didn't, however, seem to be interested in the status quo, or what other artists of that era were painting, which were mostly faces and landscapes. My vision and focus was always the sea. Later, I would find out why.

In 1971, my mom took my three brothers and me out to California to visit my Aunt Linda. Of course, I was beside myself because this was my first opportunity to see the Pacific. I'd been thinking and dreaming about it for so long and finally it happened. I remember asking the moment we got there how far it was to the ocean. My other Aunt, Terry, who was only a couple of years older than I, said it wasn't far at all, and she drove us to Laguna Beach, where I saw an expanse of blue

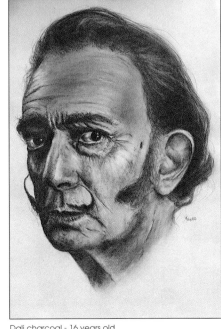

Dali charcoal - 16 years old

water that seemed to go on forever and ever.

My brothers and I immediately dove in and took a beating from the surf. It wasn't long before I realized there was something just past the first break. I saw these black backs with clusters of yellow barnacles, accompanied by magnificent sprays of water blowing up into the air. I had no idea what kind they were, but I knew I was looking at living whales for the first time. I couldn't see the entire body of each whale, only their backs coming up and blowing. But that was enough for me. I was ecstatic — I had never seen an animal that large in the wild. It was like seeing something very rare and beautiful, almost as if it were a miracle to be there when they swam by. Words alone can't describe how this first sighting impacted me, and I'll never forget what I saw that day.

It's hard to remember everything from when I was 14, but I can still see those whales today. People who have seen whales have similar stories. It's something you never forget, and I think it makes you a changed person. Obviously, I was changed by what I saw — every detail of it. I remember the yellow barnacles sparkling in the sun, and sunlit waters spraying up out of their blowholes. I remember them much more than I remember the city.

Having grown up in Detroit, I'd never seen anything like this. I told myself that one day I'd like to live here and, sure enough, 10 years later I moved to Laguna Beach and painted my first Whaling Wall mural not more than a hundred yards from the very place I'd seen those gray whales. I felt it was meant to be. Things are often meant to happen like that. How else would a kid from Detroit be so involved in this environmental movement? It took the power of a great whale to impact a 14-year-old artist for all of these things to occur.

I went back to Detroit and began to study whales in my own way. I spent a lot of time not only in the art room but in the library, diving into books and stories. I did this by not reading every story, but by looking at the pictures. As I became more and more interested in whales, dolphins and other marine mammals, I was amazed to learn there wasn't much information about them in the public libraries. The books I found relied heavily on the science of whales obtained by the history of whaling. Most of the research had been done on whales that had been killed or had washed up dead on the beach.

My first paintings of whales in 1971 were fairly primitive, but they were some of the first paintings I knew of that showed living whales in their environment. I continued to paint other things as well, but whales were imbedded in my mind's eye and were becoming an important subject in my work in the early '70s. What really cemented my commitment to whales was watching Jacques Cousteau on television. When his programs came out, I was glued to the TV. I became infatuated with the man who was out there doing what I wished I could do — traveling and studying these great creatures of the ocean. I had found my subjects. I had seen them with my own eyes a few years earlier, and here was a man calling worldwide attention to them. All of a sudden, things started clicking. I started paying more attention to my paintings, and whales started to appear in all forms in my work.

About this same time, an international group called Greenpeace was starting to make a name for itself. It consisted of a group of young environmentalists (this was the first time I'd heard the word) who were out there trying to protect whales from being hunted by the Japanese and Russians. These men and women were going out in their little boats and challenging the giant factory ships and big corporations, trying to protect an animal. It was the first time I was aware of how important the work of Greenpeace was, and I wanted to join the organization immediately. Of course, many people did. It was a pioneering time.

I kept wondering how all of these things could tie together? I was a student absorbing information. I was a big fan of Salvador Dali. I loved the surrealism he painted, and I liked the idea of his unlimited imagination. I also had a high respect for Michelangelo and his enormous talent. He did everything — sculpture, murals, paintings, everything. And Leonardo da Vinci was a genius. He was an inventor. I loved these guys, spent a lot of time studying their work and actually copied a lot of their work to learn. That was the way I would learn about a subject — I would paint it.

The environmental art movement didn't exist at that time. There were a few wildlife artists, but no marine life artists and no such thing as an environmental marine life artist. Preserving the environment was becoming more important. Before that, in the industrial age, the land was just something that man could use for his own gains or his own purposes. Nobody thought twice about dumping everything and anything into the ocean. It was just a vast, bottomless pit. But then came people like Cousteau who were

Seeing my first gray whale, Laguna Beach, CA

calling attention to it; and Greenpeace, which confronted these issues. They became imbedded in my mind's eye. I just absorbed all of this information that moved me.

As far as art in the family, my Uncle Jerry was quite an artist. He did some realistic drawings, still-life and things like that. In my early teens, I used to look up to him and think, "My God, this guy is a terrific artist." He could have had a successful art career, but he decided instead he was going to play football for the Michigan State Spartans.

I also had a great aunt, who was a renowned painter in France. Her last name was Dimitri. So, supposedly, we did have some artists in the family, but I was the only artist in the immediate family. Both of my parents were auto workers. My mom worked on the line at Chrysler, and my dad worked on the line at Chevrolet. They were very supportive of my art, though. They would come home and watch me draw for hours and hours at a time.

Probably one of the very first important influences for me was going out and meeting a professional artist named Dennis Poosch, considered by many to be the leading air brush muralist in the United States. He had a custom paint shop in Detroit, in which he painted murals on the sides of vans. My mom brought a newspaper article to my attention just as I finished working on a portfolio of paintings and illustrations that I hoped would land me a job in the art world. This was my first opportunity to meet a professional artist and show him my work.

My mom dropped me off at his studio, and I knocked on the door. When the door opened, there stood this guy who looked like he had a shrunken head, which, by the way, was the name of his company — Shrunken Head Studios. It was Dennis, an old hippie dude who had become known professionally as "Shrunken Head." I told him I'd read the newspaper article about him and wanted to meet him and possibly talk about working for him as an understudy. He looked through my portfolio and appeared impressed by the range of work I was doing.

I also found that he had a tremendous interest in Salvador Dali, and I'd done some Dali portraits. He was impressed, but at the same time he had met a lot of artists and told me a lot of them couldn't airbrush. You never touch the surface when you airbrush. You're kind of out there. I told him I felt quite confident that I could pick it up if he were my teacher.

He liked all of this optimism. I'm probably one of the most optimistic people in the world. I see hope in everything and have always believed I could do anything.

He invited me downstairs to see what he was working on. We went down to this huge shop where he had eight or nine custom vans. Some were finished and being buffed out. His work reflected a lot of Frank Frazetta and John Pitre, two great artists we both admired. Several years later, I met them both and we became good friends. The people who were commissioning these murals at the time liked the Frazetta style — the surreal fantasy. Dennis was working on this one van and had just started laying in some of the background colors. I watched him use automotive spray guns to apply the larger background colors — my first exposure to these tools. I still use them today in the majority of my outdoor murals.

He continued to spray the background colors, which actually looked like a large blur of color. There were no brush strokes. It was very smooth and had a very clean look. He would just take the cup off and mix the color in the cup, eyeballing it. I was fascinated watching this guy. He was fast and efficient. He could basically mix the color with the thinner, shake the can a few times and start spraying on the van. He was one of the fastest painters I'd ever seen. After he sprayed the background colors, he picked up his airbrush and showed it to me. It was a Pasche VL-1, a double-action airbrush. He used it unlike anyone I'd ever seen. It had a completely different look. He did everything freehand. It was very difficult, but he made it look easy. Soon I thought, "Hey, I can do this." I felt that it was drawing and painting in the same motion.

I felt myself being sucked into the energy he created with his airbrush. He worked on the van for an hour or so and, to my amazement, turned around and handed me the airbrush. I'd never had a VL in my hand before. But here was Shrunken Head, the best, handing me the baton. What he said was amazing:

"Finish it." He didn't even wait around. He just went up and had a cup of coffee and left me there. It was like someone teaching me how to swim by throwing me in the water. "Well, what the heck, it ain't my van," I said to myself. If it had been mine, I probably would have wanted to watch Dennis for a few more days.

As I started to paint, I was causing the cup to drip. I called them gravitational pulls of the earth. Also, I would spray a little too close and that would

Dad, Steve, me, mom, Bill and Tom - Atlanta, GA

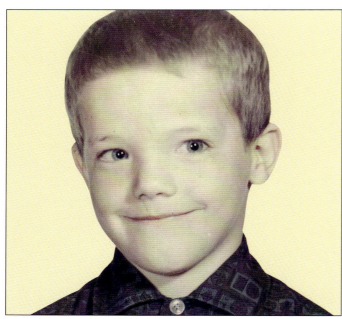
4th grade, Hoover Elementary

Brothers - Steve, Wyland, Bill, Tom

Home, Madison Heights, Michigan

cause a drip. I was having some problems, but I overcame them by painting a rock or some other thing and texturing it so you couldn't tell. After talking to Dennis later, I found that this was something he'd done as well because it is just the nature of it. There are going to be mistakes, but you just call them happy mistakes and incorporate them into the mural.

I started to get comfortable right away. At first my finger was tired, and I developed a large blister. But I stayed down there for a few hours and actually finished the mural. Dennis came down, was impressed and hired me on the spot. I'd achieved one of my goals — to work under a master artist. It was nothing new in the history of art, but it was a new experience for me. Dennis and I bonded almost like brothers, or like father and son. We respected each other, and he had me learning every aspect of the spraying equipment. I was, and still am, very grateful to Dennis Poosch.

After working with him for a few months, I told him I wanted to go out on my own and that I appreciated the time he'd spent with me. I felt it was time, and he encouraged me 100 percent. We still painted together at auto shows in Detroit, and we still get together now and then. I found that having the airbrush in my arsenal of paint tools gave me a lot more opportunities to do commercial projects. Many of my friends would ask me to do murals on the sides of their vans. In fact, the janitors in my high school would allow me to paint murals in the auto shop; they had an air compressor, which was very convenient.

Basically, I turned the whole school into my art studio. What the heck! I felt that I had access to the art room, and I'd literally paint all day until I got kicked out. We had an art teacher there, Mrs. Payne, who liked to go home as soon as school was out. Her line to me would be: "Wyland, I have to go home. I have to lock the classroom. You need to go get a life." And I said, "This is my life."

All the way through school, I'd heard of a special school in Detroit called the Society of Arts and Crafts, newly named the Center for Creative Studies. It was one of the better art schools in the country. I submitted a portfolio for a scholarship, half of which I received because of my talent, and the other half for not meeting the financial requirements.

I majored in sculpture. Painting was secondary. I loved painting, but I always thought of myself as a sculptor because I saw things three-dimensionally. I was lucky enough to work with one of the best instructors at any college in the country, Jay Holland. I'd heard that the sculpture department was tremendous, but that this guy was strict. He was a wild man who demanded full attention to details. He thought nothing of coming over to your sculpture, measuring the one-third scale model you were working on from life and, if the arms or legs were not exactly one-third to scale, he would cut those arms or legs off and throw them across the room against a brick wall, where they broke in a dozen pieces and fell into a mud bucket.

We sculpted from life, which was quite challenging. It must have been very unusual when I brought sculptures of nude men and women home. But mom got used to it. Eventually, we started doing half-scale models and then full-scale. We did heads, portraits, busts and everything. It was just terrific training. We ate, slept and drank art at this school. I could only afford, even with my scholarship, to go to so many classes, but I'd always find a way to sneak into a drawing, painting or watercolor class here and there. The instructors got to know me quite well and, knowing what my finances were, would invite me in. They kept telling me my art was a "California style." I knew that, of course, and I was biding my time. I couldn't wait to leave Michigan and the cold winters and get out to California where it was warm, the art was vibrant and fresh and people weren't afraid to try new things. I knew exactly where I wanted to be; I just didn't know how it was going to happen.

In college, I worked with some great instructors, like Bill Gerard, my mentor in painting. He taught me the old master style of glazing and everything else from A to Z. He also taught me the idea that art is fun and an expression of your own personal spirit. He reminded me of someone of the Rembrandt period, the classic fine artist. He had a very gentle spirit, and his main purpose was to nurture artists and help them develop. He was the classic fine artist.

The other guy I admired so much was Russell Keeter. Russell was even more wild — a free spirit. He had attended school at the Ringling School of Art in Sarasota, Florida. He was another mentor for me because he was

Bad hair day, Wyland top right

5th grade

9th grade basketball team - #10, Page Jr. High

First mural - Dairy Queen, Detroit 1973

10th grade art class

Airbrushing custom van murals 1972

Master airbrush artist/teacher Dennis Poosch Shrunken Head Studios - Detroit

kind of a surrealist guy. He wasn't like Dali, though. He had a style that was uniquely his own. He developed a lot of original paintings that dealt with different types of surrealism.

Russell was also a realist and could paint anything. He taught the life drawing classes and was considered one of the best in the country at drawing figures. He would take the entire class and a model to the top of a building in Detroit, weather permitting, and we would paint the model in the landscape of the inner city. It was fun for everybody. He was also very supportive of my work because I was a very serious artist.

Russell Keeter's only downside was that he didn't like the business of art. He felt that a fine artist shouldn't consider business. That's where we kind of bumped heads because I said, "Hey, how are you supposed to pay for your art supplies? How are you supposed to pay for your life?" He felt that your art was the most important and you shouldn't be thinking about business. Many years later, I would visit Russell in Detroit, and he asked me if I would lecture his class on the business of art. He knew I'd gone through the school of hard knocks and become successful not only in my painting in California, but in the marketing and selling of my own work.

I was happy to lecture his students, who were very eager to learn. Today, more art schools have business classes for artists. I'm starting to see more of that in colleges where I lecture. It's really nice to see because this is a complete picture for the artist. If the artist doesn't at least understand and appreciate business, then it's only a partial career. To be successful in art, you have to understand not only being a fine artist, but a fine businessman as well. If you don't want to do your business and market and sell your art, you at least have to know how it's done so you can make decisions on how you want your work to be sold and so forth. It's very, very important. There is no doubt that the most important thing is creating the art. But you have to know everything else that is available to the artist. In my opinion, this is the best time in history to be an artist because you can actually make a living. Many more people are actually collecting art. Not just the wealthy, like in the old days. Regular people can collect art, too — limited editions, posters, paintings. Everybody seems to have an appreciation for art. There's a tremendous opportunity for the artist today that wasn't there in the past.

After leaving Dennis Poosch, I was approached by one of my physical education teachers, Don Huffsinger. He had just purchased a Dairy Queen as a business in Royal Oak, Michigan. He had a big blank ugly wall. He approached me and said, "Hey, Wyland, I just bought this building and have a big wall. Would you be interested in painting a mural?" I immediately said yes because I wanted to

Sea Captain Mural - California 1977

High school record - high jump 1974

Dad, artist, mom

Track team captain 1973, front row, center

Original Above and Below painting 1971

paint a mural. He said he had a budget of $300. At the time, that was pretty good.

Don was going to buy the paint and supplies and asked me if I would do a mountain scene. So I looked through some books and found one of the Alps. I hadn't painted any murals on that scale. This was a pretty big wall, probably 100 feet long and 18 feet high. I really didn't know how to approach it, so I went to the library. But there were no books on how to paint a mural. So, when I saw the ladders Don had provided, I thought to myself: "It's really only a large painting, nothing more." Dennis Poosch had shown me how to use spray guns, and I decided to paint it like I would a smaller mural. I started blocking in the color in masses and covered up the wall in a short time. Eventually, I started carving out the mountains. I learned how to control the spray gun to put in small details. Along with everyone else, I was amazed at how fast the mural progressed. I finished it in three days, when Don thought it would take three weeks. I didn't do any preliminary drawings or grids, which I later found out most artists like to do. I just started painting like I would a smaller painting. To my amazement, everything just started developing like a Polaroid photograph, where you see this blur of color slowly coming into sharp focus.

Oil painting demonstration

Center for Creative Studies, College of Art and Design - Detroit 1976

After I'd blocked in a lot of the colors for the mountains and reflections of the color of the sky, I used my smaller airbrush, my Pasche, to paint in some of the details. I also used some of my brushes to give it sharp edges. When it was done, it drew a lot of attention. People stopped to take pictures of the mural and to buy ice cream. Needless to say, Don was ecstatic.

I then began getting requests to do other murals. The Meat Market in Royal Oak had seen the Dairy Queen and requested that I do one on the side of the market wall. They gave me a photograph of a heifer in a field and, again, I just went up and painted a mural in two days. It was turning out to be quite a good business. It also was a good learning experience. I was practicing on other people's walls. I was very loose, and sometimes that's when you do your best work. Suddenly, someone in almost every neighborhood in the city wanted me to paint a mural on the side of their garage door. I would paint one, and another neighbor would walk along and see how beautiful it was and ask if I could do a mural on their garage door. It was a wonderful experience that I later used to paint the murals I'm doing now of the whales.

It was a great beginning.

As a child I was fascinated by stories and pictures of that great ocean creature, the whale. My interest deepened while I was filming "Sea Hunt" because of my close association with the sea and my experiences with the dolphins.

When I saw the beauty and shared the emotion of Wyland's art, my appreciation of the whale increased.

My son Beau and I were making a movie in Arizona and visited the Biosphere, a huge and amazing environmental experiment. To our delight we found Wyland there, painting one of his magnificent Whaling Walls. Beau had met Wyland previously, so we rated a personal greeting and were allowed to paint a few strokes on the mural, which not only scared us, (in case we made a mistake), but also made us feel quite important.

Before it's too late we must do what we can to save the endangered whales and dolphins. Among the organizations devoted to this cause are Earthtrust and Whales Alive, both located in Hawaii. Join me and my family in this needed effort.

Thank you Wyland, for making the world more aware and more caring.

Lloyd Bridges

With favorite actor, Paul Newman

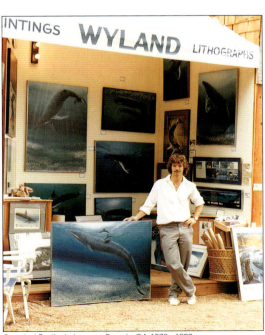

Sawdust Festival - Laguna Beach, CA 1979 - 1992

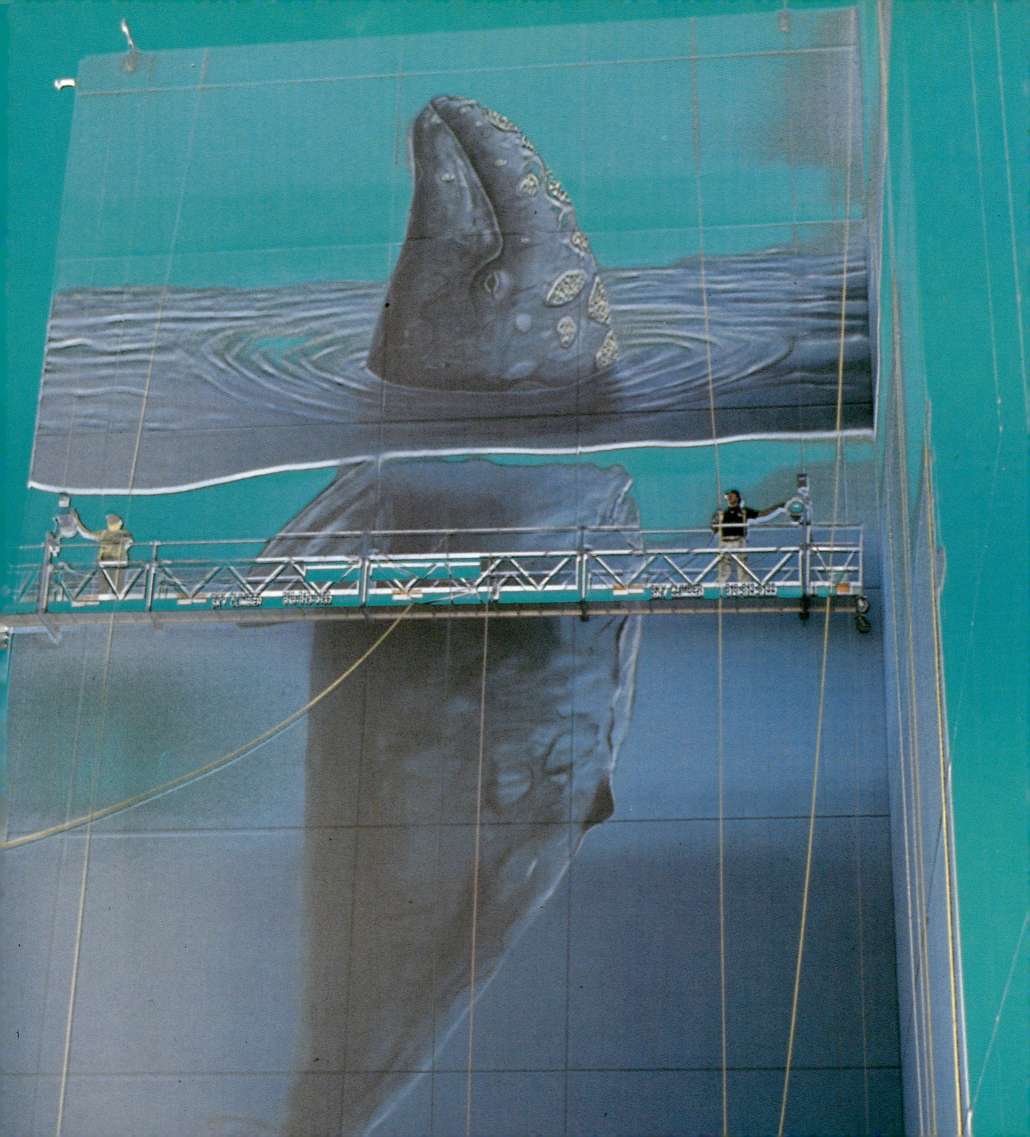

II
THE ART OF SAVING WHALES

27

...You don't have to live on the ocean to want to protect it...

▲ Painting orcas - Victoria, B.C., Canada 1985

Early two worlds painting 1972

Original oil paintings 1978

I was once asked by *People* magazine how painting a whale on a wall could save a whale. I still believe today that it may well be the only thing that can.

I hope that the many people who view my murals will be inspired to learn more about whales. Most people don't expect to be driving down the road and suddenly encounter life-size whales. But when they encounter a Whaling Wall, they're impacted in a way that's the next best thing to actually seeing the whales up close in the wild.

I've said for many years that when you see a whale, you become a changed person. Certainly that was the case when I saw my first whale. Even though I only saw a small portion of a gray whale as it passed by the Laguna Beach, California shore, the image was so powerful that I still reflect it in my work today. Over the years, I've met many people who have had similar experiences, all of whom were equally inspired and some who have gone on to crusade for these gentle giants.

The El Neuvo Reino Aventura in Mexico City has agreed to release Keiko - Free Willy - to a larger habitat within 12-18 months with the painting of Wyland's historic Whaling Wall, September, 1994

For me, plain and simple, the idea to paint these whales in their true life-size developed out of the difficulty of trying to capture their awesome size and majesty on smaller canvases. I needed larger canvases so I started looking at the sides of walls. . . Whaling Walls.

My desire to paint whales began as early as 1971. The paintings at that time were very primitive. And, as I began to research libraries, I found that most of the information about whales had been gathered from whales that had been killed for the whaling industry or that had happened up on various beaches from whale strandings. The problem was that, visually, these animals were far from anatomically correct. If a whale was found on a shoreline, the weight of the animal would distort the way it had actually looked living and breathing in its ocean environment.

As a result, whales were a mystery for hundreds of years. Most had only been seen by the very people who were hunting them. Whales were only considered a product, not the product of beauty like they are today. To add

Above and Below painting 1977

Laguna Beach studio with favorite painting, Children of the Sea

With artist/author Richard Ellis at Orange County Marine Institute - Dana Point, CA

Artist with Bob Hunter - Greenpeace founder

Life-size gray whales - Whiterock, B.C., Canada

First life-size bronze sculpture - Synchronicity 1992

Working on stone lithograph

to the myth, early paintings of whales depicted them as monsters. Even *Moby Dick* was created as a very aggressive and dangerous animal. We know today that nothing could be further from the truth.

It has only been in the last 20 years that people have begun to understand *living* whales. In fact, until 10 years ago, there was not one photograph of a living blue whale. Fortunately, in the early '70s, due to a handful of pioneers — like Jacques Cousteau, Dr. Roger Payne and a dedicated few — the era of whale research began. And shortly thereafter, a small group of committed volunteers organized the first campaign to save the whales. Greenpeace confronted the whaling issue head-on in a political battle and, like David and Goliath, took on and nearly defeated the powerful commercial whaling industry. These individuals and groups inspired an entire generation. I, for one, as a young artist, had found my subject.

To be honest, my paintings back then were seen as very peculiar. And, for a number of years, I couldn't give them away. I was the classic starving artist. But, as the world's environmental consciousness grew, so did appreciation for my work. I personally was obsessed with learning everything I could about whales and dolphins and other marine life. I also felt a need to help these animals, who desperately needed to attract attention to their plight. Something about the ocean and its creatures moved me to a higher level of consciousness. I was compelled to try and do something for these great whales, and I had to find a way.

I had seen the way my paintings communicated not only the power of whales, but also the great spirit they possess. Then, one day it hit me like a bolt of lightning — I needed to paint these living whales life-size in their own environment. I knew that if I could paint a 45-foot gray whale on an outdoor wall in a public place, many more people would see the unique beauty of these creatures.

The first day I painted a life-size whale on a wall in Laguna Beach, it caused such a commotion that the Police Department was worried about traffic accidents. The crowds were enormous, and I found that the entire city was talking about whales. As I added barnacles and other details to

With artist Frank Frazetta and wife Ellie

Painting on Front Street Dolphin Gallery, Lahaina, Maui 1981

With wildlife artist Robert Bateman - Victoria, B.C., Canada 1985

With singer/songwriter Dan Fogelberg

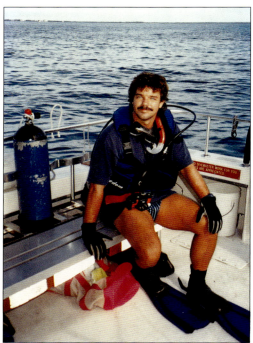
Diving

With Lloyd and Beau Bridges at Biosphere II - Arizona 1993

The Wyland Studio's gang, Laguna Beach

the whale, I realized, along with the crowds of people watching, just how large and magnificent these animals really are.

The best part for me was painting the eye and realizing through this experience the emotional impact this giant painting had. By this time, the mural had become a gathering place for people who cared about whales. To my surprise, the mural attracted people from two years old to 90, and everyone in between. The transformation of this ugly blank wall into a beautiful blue cutaway of the Pacific Ocean, with a mother gray whale and her calf, became not only a piece of art, but a classroom by the sea.

After completing that first mural in Laguna Beach, I knew that if I could continue to paint a number of these murals in different cities around the world, I could indeed make a difference. I told a reporter at the dedication of that first mural, on my 25th birthday, that I would paint 100 of these

Whaling Walls around the world to create awareness — not only for the whales, but for the endangered oceans in which they live.

So far, I've completed over 67 different Whaling Walls throughout the U.S., Canada, Japan, Australia and Europe. In the 15 years since I painted my first wall, I've seen a tremendous increase in people's awareness, not only in the U.S., but in other countries as well. It is estimated that the Whaling Walls are seen by over one billion people annually. I'm often asked if my work is making a difference. Fortunately, I've been doing it long enough to see that it has.

Hardly a week goes by when I don't receive a number of letters, paintings and drawings from kids who were inspired by the Whaling Walls to continue on the path of consciousness and not convenience. If one kid grows up to be a Jacques Cousteau, then I will feel all of my efforts will have been worth it.

Coming into Honolulu from the airport the other day I bolted up in my seat at the sight of this huge blue wall. I commanded my driver to circle over so this unexpected mirage could be viewed in its entirety.

Imagine the excitement when I discovered immense, life-size whales swirling and zipping about.

What a tremendous imaginative undertaking, so in keeping with the environment, what great subject matter and how capably and beautifully this talented, daring, young artist has so boldly tied into this awesome task.

Bravo! It will be a tourist attraction, residents will love it, lovers of sea life will identify with it and children for generations to come will experience it with wide eyes.

Congratulations Wyland.

LeRoy Neiman

Collaborating with dolphin artist - Dolphin Research Center 1990

THE FIRST WHALING WALL

...Some have said, "How can a painting of a whale on a wall save them?" I believe it may very well be the only thing that can...

▲ Whaling Wall I - Laguna Beach, CA 1981

THE WHAL

Laguna Beach wall before mural

Background colors

Artist

▲ Laguna Beach Whaling Wall completed 1981

ING WALL

Finished mural 1981

Gray whale flukes

Repainted mural 1986

...Whaling Walls are life-size tributes to living whales...

My mom decided in 1971 to take my brothers and me to California to visit my Aunt Linda. She loaded the four of us in the car and across country we went.

As soon as we got to Los Angeles, my mom's youngest sister, Terry, scooped us all up and drove us out to Laguna Beach. This was a beautiful little art community and an internationally known art colony — a true Gallery Row. I would come to find out later that many towns have their own sign of the Zodiac. Laguna's sign was the same as mine — Cancer, the water sign. To me, it was a magical place.

Here was a kid who had dreamed about the ocean his entire life, and there it was, right in front of me. I immediately ran out into the water and just drank up the whole scene. Just as I looked back at Aunt Terry on the beach, a giant wave pounded me face first into the sand, rolling and tumbling me back onto the beach. Welcome to the Pacific Ocean! I jumped right back in, though. I was finally in a real ocean, with real salt water and sand! As I swam, I glanced out to sea and saw some huge creatures swimming no more than 100 yards off the beach, just past the waves. Wiping the salt water out of my eyes, I focused in on the creatures and, to my great amazement, realized that these were whales! These were the great California gray whales I had read so much about, migrating down the Pacific Coast to the warm breeding grounds of Mexico. There I was, my first time in the ocean, and the greatest creatures in the ocean just happened to swim by, blowing in the water just a short swim away. I mean, what are the chances of something like that happening?

I watched the whales swim on down the coast until I couldn't see them any longer and, when my head cleared, I realized I'd seen something I was meant to see.

After returning to Detroit and finishing high school, I studied sculpture and painting at the Center for Creative Studies College. Primarily, I was painting classical figures and sculpting. The

First Whaling Wall 1981

whole time, however, I found my mind and my palette leaning toward the ocean. I decided after these two years of very hard, cold winters that my destiny was to be in California. I had to follow my dream, so, in 1976, I decided to pack up the brushes in my old custom van and drive out to California. I headed straight for Laguna Beach and got a little apartment, a tiny hole in the wall. This would be my studio, where I began selling my paintings. I wasn't really worried about becoming some super-rich artist. I was content having a roof over my head, some brushes and paint. That, to me, was being a professional artist.

As I painted more and more to make a living, I began to realize that something was driving me to look for larger canvasses. I was feeling contained, basically. Then, one day it hit me like a lightning bolt. "Hey, I've got to paint these things on walls," I said out loud to myself. I had done murals, lots of 'em. In a flash, it all clicked. If I was going to paint these whales as they really are, I should paint them life-size. So I began to look for walls. I think I scouted the entire West Coast. I drove all the way from San Diego to San Francisco, charting and photographing blank walls.

One day in 1977, coming home to Laguna and stuck in traffic, I spotted this giant wall on Pacific Coast Highway. When I saw it, I envisioned a pod of gray whales migrating along with the traffic. Anyone driving by couldn't possibly miss this wall. They'd see it and become inspired by the size, beauty, intelligence and unique quality these animals have. I thought it would be a unique way to do something to help save whales. There was Greenpeace in their Zodiaks, and Cousteau with his beautiful inspiring films and documentaries. And now here was something I could do. From that day on, I called my work the Art of Saving Whales. I was only one artist, but with the ability to paint life-size whales on a large scale, I thought I could get people's attention and impact them.

Everything sort of came to me at once, as it usually does. The term "Whaling Wall" just came out of my mouth, simple, whales on walls, right? I didn't even think about the *Wailing Wall* in Jerusalem. But the symbolism is contagious; whales are very special, some of God's greatest creatures. Why not worship whales? Man's long history of thinking of the animals as being there only for his use is one of mankind's greatest tragedies. Whales are a product of beauty worthy of protection, and the Whaling Walls are a celebration of living whales. They're gathering

L.A. Times reporter after city council hearing - Laguna Beach 1979

First Whaling Wall site, Pacific Coast Hwy - Laguna Beach 1978

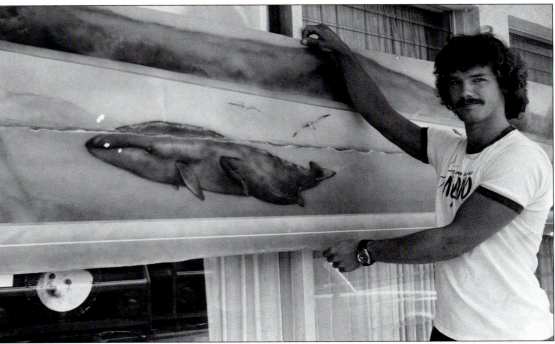
Rendering for Pacific Coast Hwy mural, Laguna Beach

Art For Whales' Sake

Jerusalem is famous for its Wailing Wall where Jews have traditionally gathered for centuries to pray. Laguna Beach may soon become famous for its Whaling Wall where artist Robert Wyland hopes to paint a marine scene featuring California Grey Whales, porpoises and sea lions.

The young muralist may be one of few people who can be awe-inspired by a blank wall. But the 300-foot concrete fence situated along Coast Highway between High and Myrtle streets is an artist's dream-come-true, he says.

"I looked at that wall and I saw a whale," said the 23-year-old Newport Beach resident. "And when you think of whales, you think of Greenpeace."

Wyland approached Greenpeace's Huntington Beach office with the plan — an artistic tribute to sea mammals. Jeff Utigard of Greenpeace contacted the City of Laguna Beach who, in turn, referred him to the California Department of Transportation.

The bureaucratic process is beginning to wear at the artist's resolve.

"I've been working on this idea for over a year now," says Wyland, "and I hope it happens soon before I use up all my enthusiasm. You can only keep that energy level going for so long."

Hopefully, he says, the waiting won't longer. The Laguna Beach Arts proved the plan. The next approval.

The wall 7 feet at turn the ground of

The proce the wall and says. Then b help him pri water seal.

A base coat by acrylic lacq lights, and a fin finish

"I could finish the whole project in four because I don't do any brush work," the artist tains. "That's about five times faster than any muralist works."

Wyland knows whereof he speaks. His mural enhanced the coast of Orange County from Dan to Huntington Beach, and he has seven years of ence airbrushing designs on vans. He currently the Newport Art School of Free-Hand Airbru

"I think free-hand airbrushing gives a muc realistic effect. I have to do the best job I ca one because it will be going into an art colony will be open to a lot of criticism from a lot of a hope they'll just see it as one artist's point-of

Arthur Van Ryhn of Cal Trans has seen W point of view, and he agrees with it. Part of his the state is to approve art for sites under C management. Since the Laguna Beach sidewalk's width from a state hi category

"I like to se to inspect

(Register Photo By CATHY LAWHON)

Artist Robert Wyland Plans Marine Mural For Laguna Beach
His Artwork Appears In Various Locations Around Orange County

---

Laguna Council Torpedoes W

Distraction for Drivers Feared

Los Angeles Times Part II / Thursday, December 4, 1980

By GORDON GRANT, *Times Staff Writer*

Plans for a 350-foot marine mural on a blank wall along Laguna Beach's Coast Highway have gone down the drain.

City Council members have decided that the mural might create a traffic hazard by distracting drivers.

The unanimous vote against the project came Tuesday night, despite the fact the artist, Robert Wyland, had previously had enthusiastic approval of other city officials, the Arts Commission, and the state Department of Transportation, which owns the wall.

Ironically, city Fire Department crews had helped wash down the wall just a few days before in preparation for the first primer coats.

"Right up to the last minute, we thought we had it made," Wyland said.

But Mayor Wayne Baglin, after hearing protests from members of the North Laguna Community Assn, who brought up the question of possible traffic dangers, led the opposition and, to the surprise of half a hundred mural supporters at the meeting who had expected at least a split vote, carried the other four council members with him.

Wyland, 24, who has created other large murals along the coast and who p poises and other m called his "Whal looking for anoth

"I spent ever Laguna to be n into it to just le He also sta Irving Bowl ing.

"It was but adde whateve City posed

His Whaling Wall Awaits

Robert Wyland is seeking support to transform a wall along Coast Highway in Lagu

By GORDON GRANT, *Times Staff Writer*

350-foot-long concrete wall — a dead, blank along Coast Highway in for 48 years — will come to ts the support of enough

ne mural, domi- California gray porpoises,

rt Wyland, approval of a Beach Arts om Greenpeace, ntal organization. ve clearance from there early. He's cleaned up an air compressor in hand leaning against the wall of the the wall," he said.

"But they've gotten some protests, so we're not home free yet."

Wyland, who has done other outdoor murals along the coast, said he began looking for a wall big enough to accommodate a whale — a "Whaling Wall," he laughed — more than a year ago.

The one in Laguna Beach seemed ideal. It is longer than a football field, stretching between High Drive and Myrtle Street. It is 14 feet high at one end, tapering to 7 feet at the other. It was built in 1932 as a retaining wall.

The Laguna Beach Fire Department has scrubbed it clean, Wyland has made scaled renditions and now he is trying to raise an estimated $10,000 to pay for the project.

He said he has arranged for a benefit concert on Nov. 30 at the Irvine Bowl and has commitments from four bands to donate the music. They are Dick Dale, Joseph Nicoletti's Bush Band, Rod Piazza and the Chicago Flying Saucers.

"They'll give us surf, rock and blues," he said. "Somet one."

If the benefit is successful, he said he would start work the next day, painting 12 hours a day, seven days a week — weather permitting — and be finished just before Christmas. He would use graffiti-res

See MUR

WALL...

s trying to work out the parking lot owners, adding that the longer if takes he wall, the deeper he'll go in debt. tributions to only $500 and all that came from one ple. I'm still accepting donations, ns — I'm really going in the hole with this thing," even if he doesn't break even with the mural, he it's worth the effort.

HIS MAIN CONCERNS are the preservation of whales and sealife and the presentation of art in public places, especially Laguna Beach.

When the predominantly turquoise, blue and gray mural is completed, it will show a 60-foot gray whale and her calf, a couple of dolphins, some sea lions on a rock, and detail work "authentic down to the barnacles,"

Wyland says.

If you're interested in seeing the artist at work, and maybe tossing a couple of bucks his way, you can find him 20 feet off the ground, leaning against the wall of the Fahrenheit 451 bookstore. He'll be there early. He's cleaned up But you'd better get there early. He's cleaned up gone by mid-morning.

WHALE: Mu

Continued from First Page

them in payment for paints a But what he calls his "Wh last airbrush strokes went o Wyland's 25th birthday.

A mother whale, 60 feet blow, while her 20-foot cal poises, a school of bonita Garibaldi perch — all life of sea lions basks on a rock

Wyland, who already Orange County Marine In other seafaring murals alo ideas.

"I want to do a life species of whales in cou said. "I want to start in humpback whales play

"Then in other pa whales, sperm whales whales.

"This one in Lagu

Daily Pilot

ORANGE COAST
THURSDAY, MAY 7, 1981

ORANGE COUNTY, CALIFORNIA — YOUR HOMETOWN DAILY PAPER — 25 CENTS

eached whale
...na artist fights clock, funds ...mplete 170-foot-long mural

ORANGE COUNTY
Los Angeles Times

Local News / Editorial Page

...al Represents a ...ale of a Struggle

Robert Wyland presents the gray whale that is the central subject of his 170-foot mural on a wall above the parking lot of the Ho...

TOM TALKS
by Tom Klingenmeier (October 1981)

Wyland's desire to create his Whaling Wall collided head-on with local politics. As a reporter for a weekly newspaper, I started covering his story and became enraged at what I saw happening.

When I first met Wyland, he had already secured the necessary endorsements from civic and social leaders, and the encroachment permit from CalTrans to put the mural on a wall they owned and maintained at the north end of town.

The North Laguna Community Association, a small group of citizens, got word of the proposed mural, and thinking it would depict angry raised fists in bright reds and oranges, decided to make it a public issue. They were joined by another neighborhood group who had been trying, unsuccessfully, for several years to get a stoplight and crosswalk at the north end of the proposed mural site. The mural became a lever to achieve their goals by forcing the issue before the City Council.

Wyland was invited to attend the Community Association's public meeting by the pro-mural members, in an effort to dispel the fears of those concerned with the potential subject of the mural. The meeting had been termed a "routine formality" for Wyland, and should have been the last step in securing the site. CalTrans officials also attended to let the community know "there was no increase in traffic accidents at any of their other mural sites."

The tone of the small gathering soon turned from one of acceptance of the young artist to art censorship, as a few elderly citizens made reference to "the local beauty of our trees, flowers and sunsets" as being the only kind of "free art" Laguna Beach needed.

The political maneuvering emerged as they combined these feelings with their own demands for traffic safety. The matter now had to go before the City Council.

I couldn't believe what I was witnessing. This was an internationally known artist colony, and they were trying to use censorship and politics to refuse a man his right to make a statement and provide free art in a public place.

places for people who care about them and all life in the sea.

I decided that in order to proceed, I'd have to find out who owned the building. I went to Greenpeace right off, thinking they might help me because they were involved with saving whales. They loved it immediately and proceeded to find out whose approval I needed and who might be willing to help pay for paint and provide equipment. At this point, I had no concept of the bureaucracy involved with a project like this. I never dreamed that to paint a public mural would require me to become embroiled in a three-year quagmire of politics and red tape.

Greenpeace eventually gave up, threw in the towel. This was a good indication of the level of politics involved. Greenpeace? International Goliath-killers? Normally, they never give in. We had to attend countless city meetings. Cal Trans backed us initially and were supportive, but the city was where it started getting ugly. The mayor of Laguna Beach, Wayne Baglan, was opposed to it for reasons no one was ever sure of. To this day, I think it was because it wasn't his idea, a situation I still run into on occasion. I had to agree that this was a unique project. There were no public murals in Laguna — a city rich in art history — no outdoor murals. To me it was a natural. I mean, here's a coastal city; here's the ocean; here are the gray whales, the state marine mammal for goodness sake. There *was* no better place; it was just common sense. I learned pretty quickly, though, that common sense doesn't always get you there, especially at city hall. I was about to learn that in order for me to publicly share the Art of Saving Whales, I would first have to learn the politics of painting public murals.

I already had the blessing of the owner of the wall, Cal Trans, but only if the city agreed first. So I went to the city, accompanied by Greenpeace and the Laguna Beach Arts Commission, who both made tremendous presentations. Most of the officials liked it, but the mayor managed somehow to convince some of the city council members it was not a good idea for Laguna.

We went to meetings for two years, and they kept putting it off. Finally, a group called the North Laguna Community Association decided to use my wall as a political vehicle to get a traffic light installed in their community. I went to one of the association's meetings to explain the details of the mural. This was the final approval we needed to get the city council to vote in our favor. But it was a complete setup. The association shot the project down from every angle possible.

It came down to one final city council meeting where three of the five council members told me point blank that they were in favor of the mural and that it was going to pass. When it came time to make the final presentation to the council, there was a lot of really emotional testimony as to why this mural was important. A couple of North Laguna Community Association members testified as well, saying "Hey, this Wyland is not even from Laguna Beach. He wasn't born here," and "Why doesn't he paint the whales being harpooned?" I couldn't believe my ears on that one. The idea of painting living whales didn't appeal to them. They wanted more action — they wanted to see some people slaughtering whales!

The city council voted against it — all of them. It had been three years since I had first approached the city for approval. I was absolutely committed to this wall and had spent every dime I had, roughly $20,000. It wasn't easy to paint and earn a living when I was constantly attending meetings and making presentations. I was totally dejected, three years of my life down the drain.

Heartbroken, I walked out of city hall and started toward my old, beat-up car. Suddenly, Tom Klingenmeier, a reporter from a local paper called *The Tides and Times* walked up, put his arm around me and said, "Look, Wyland, I've been following this for three years, and I gotta tell you — I'm from Chicago and they have murals there that were very well received. Don't give up. This thing is worth fighting for."

Less than 48 hours later, I decided I would just find another wall, and that's exactly what I did. There was another wall on Pacific Coast Highway, which I had seen before I located the first wall. It was on private property, the Hotel Laguna, one of the oldest hotels in Laguna. Plus, the owner was very receptive. I'd learned something about the process of approvals, so I gave it another try. Much to my surprise, the city said yes immediately. They were sick of looking at me, I guess. Either that or I wore 'em out. This time, I needed permission from the Laguna Design Review, which I didn't know, and from the Laguna Arts Council. I wasn't worried about the Arts Council because they were already for it.

The vote among the Design Review was close: two in favor, two opposed, one on the fence. The guy on the fence was a guy named Dan Kenney, and I remember him staring at me, trying to decide if he should really do this. He looked at me for a long time and finally said, "I have reservations. . . I'm not sure I should do this, but. . . okay."

We'd won! The next morning, I was down there at 7:00. I painted with real passion because I had a mission. The wall now has a mother gray whale and her calf making their way past Laguna Beach on their way from the Bering Sea to Baja, Mexico. It turned out to be a major art event for the city as I painted. The crowds were enormous. People were pulling their cars over and creating huge traffic jams. And, that's what I wanted. This was an event, a vehicle to show people how beautiful these animals are and that they are worthy of protection. That's when I decided I would do 100 Whaling Walls. I thought if I could make that big of an impact with one mural, what could I do if I painted 100?

Four years later, the city asked me to come to City Hall — the same people who had earlier shot me down — to give me a resolution award for my work and ask me to do another mural. In an indirect manner, they tried to explain their earlier denial as a situation where everyone was scared of change.

I guess that was what it was all about — fear of the unknown. I myself have seen a lot of horrible murals, and how were they to know this wouldn't be another one? But I believe everything happens for a reason, and this Whaling Wall was meant to be from the time I took that first swim off Laguna Beach and saw my first gray whale. The mural has become one of Southern California's favorite landmarks, photographed by tens of thousands of people each year. For me, it marked the start of a much greater work — the first of 100 Whaling Walls I'm painting around the world. For Laguna Beach, I think it might have marked the beginning of a new medium in that city's art history and created a new sensitivity toward whale-size art in public places.

I abandoned all the rules of good newspaper reporting, especially the one about not creating the news, just reporting it, and urged Wyland to do everything in his power to achieve his goal. I helped him gather signatures, hold art shows to display his mutual rendering and inform the public of the issues, and sold posters announcing his project. I believed that thousands of signatures on petitions in support of the mural would convince the City Council members that the majority of the community wanted the mural. I had so many meetings with Wyland and late night phone calls, that my wife was thinking of suing the young muralist for alienation of my affections. But, I was just as determined as Wyland to see the project completed.

Wyland attended the City Council meeting carrying his petitions, with over 2,000 signatures, and packed their chambers with supporters at one of the largest meetings ever held.

The mayor and other council members opened the hearing by stating they hadn't realized just how big the mural was, when it was first brought to their attentions. (Wyland had initially taken a rendering to the City Manager with all the specifications and received a letter from him stating the city couldn't get involved since the wall belonged to CalTrans, but "we're looking forward to seeing it done.") The Council further stated they felt there would be a traffic hazard at the site, in spite of CalTrans' official report to the contrary.

Wyland tried to convince the council that he should indeed be allowed to complete the project. But, we hadn't counted on the vote-getting power of the North Laguna community members. The council members responded to this small, but powerful minority and unanimously rejected the mural.

Wyland left that meeting a very bitter young man and went into a self-imposed exile to re-evaluate his priorities. I remained determined.

We had several meetings after that evening and became more obsessed with painting that mural on a wall in Laguna Beach. Wyland located another wall on private property and came to me for help once again. I carried this rendering back to City Hall and asked for the correct procedure to obtain the permits necessary to paint it on a private parking lot site, at the Laguna Hotel. I was informed it only had to pass the town's Design Review Board, a group of five citizens charged with "maintaining a village atmosphere," and wait for an appeal period before he could begin the project.

Wyland approached the first board meeting with great trepidation. One of the members was absent, and the rest of the board quickly made their feelings known. One member would vote against it because of safety reasons. Another no vote would come from a member, who was opposed to any art in public places, and the other two members were in favor of the project.

I urged Wyland to come back to the next meeting (a tie vote is the same as no vote), and we went to work securing more information to convince the panel of the wall's merit.

We met several times at the new site and measured distances from traffic signals, crosswalks and parking spaces. We took pictures of the proposed site from every conceivable angle to persuade the board members that this site was completely safe and aesthetically perfect for his art.

With the nervous feeling that accompanied a teenager on his first date, I followed Wyland into the second meeting. He made the presentation and returned to his seat to allow the board to discuss the project. The original four were still evenly split, and the entire gathering turned to the now present fifth member. He asked a few pertinent questions and called for a vote. Wyland had his mural and I had a fantastic story. ✷

IV
WHALING WALLS

...When you work for free you gotta work fast...

▲ *The Norfolk Compass,* August 22, 1993

WHALING WALL 1
GRAY WHALES

Wyland's idea for painting whales on the sides of buildings developed quite naturally from the difficulty he was having in portraying the mammoth creatures on small canvasses. In 1978, his desire to paint whales life-size led him up and down the Pacific Coast Highway from San Diego to San Francisco until he finally found the "perfect wall" in Laguna Beach.

Laguna's long history as an internationally known art colony, its coastal location and the fact that the gray whales migrate along its shoreline each year made it the best choice for Wyland's first life-size mural.

Depicting a life-size California gray whale and her calf, the mural was completed on the side of the Hotel Laguna on July 9, 1981. The dedication ceremony was held amid great public adulation and considerable fanfare. And it also happened to be Wyland's 25th birthday.

"While I was finishing this mural, I realized the kind of impact it was having on the people who were looking at it," he says. "There was nothing like it in Orange County, or anywhere else for that matter. The public's response was just fantastic, and this was when I decided to paint 100 of these Whaling Walls throughout the world."

Five years later, Wyland returned to repaint Whaling Wall I because cars from the hotel's parking lot were continually bumping into it. While refurbishing the wall, he surprised everyone by repainting the whales so that they faced the opposite direction, toward the ocean.

"I just wanted the public to view the mural in a new perspective," he says of the reversal. "People told me something looked different, but they couldn't figure out what it was."

Laguna Beach

Wall before mural

▲ 1981 Whaling Wall I — Laguna Beach, California — 140 feet long x 26 feet high — Dedicated July 9, 1981 by Mrs. John Wayne

First Wyland Wall 1981

California sea lions on rock

From Quinn Inouye, age 9

WHALING WALL 2
YOUNG GRAY WHALE

After seeing Wyland's first Whaling Wall in Laguna Beach, the director of the Orange County Marine Institute, Dr. Stan Cummings, asked Wyland if he would paint a mural at the institute in Dana Point, California.

Upon visiting the facility in 1982, the artist was struck by the skeleton of a young gray whale suspended from the ceiling. It was a gray whale that had washed ashore in 1980 in Huntington Beach and had been reconstructed and placed on display.

"I immediately wanted to paint that whale as if it was living, and in its true size, so that one could look up at the wall and relate the bones to the exterior anatomy," Wyland recalls. "I think this is another idea where art and science can work together to achieve a higher purpose. Students at the institute can now study the living whale alongside the skeleton and gain a much better understanding of these mammals."

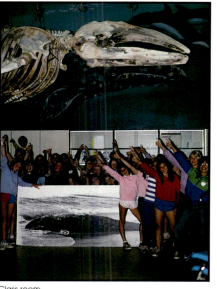

Class room

WHALING WALL 3
SPYHOPPING

When Wyland was asked to paint a mural at Marineland in Palos Verdes, California, he had his choice of walls. After walking by one wall that he found rather interesting because of its height, he walked out to the peninsula that overlooks Palos Verdes.

Just as he looked out over the bay, a gray whale stuck its head completely out of the water in a behavior called "spyhopping." The whale, and the wall he had viewed minutes earlier, suddenly came together in his mind. "At that moment, I had my painting," Wyland says. "It was just a matter of creating it. The image was there."

It took nine days for Wyland to complete the 20'x30' mural, which is located in the park's whale pavilion. "The interesting thing about painting at Marineland was that there were so many people watching me work," the artist says. "It was a lot of fun and very inspirational to talk to all of them about their different experiences with whales. I think we all learned something."

▲ 1982 Whaling Wall II — Orange County Marine Institute, Dana Point, California — 45 feet long x 10 feet high — Dedicated March 20, 1982 by Bill Toomey, Olympic Decathalon Champion

Whaling Wall III — Marineland, Rancho Palos Verdes, California — 20 feet long x 30 feet high — Dedicated June 27, 1984. By Cleveland Amory, FUND FOR ANIMALS

Painting barnacle

50

First whale crossing sign

...Breath of life...breath of whales...

▲ 1984 Whaling Wall IV — White Rock, British Columbia, Canada — 70 feet long x 30 feet high — Dedicated September 29, 1984 by Gordon Hogg, Mayor of White Rock

WHALING WALL 4
THE GRAY WHALE FAMILY

In 1984, the mayor of White Rock, Canada, Gordon Hogg, was looking for public art. The death of seven gray whales that year in the White Rock area had alarmed the community and heightened their awareness of the animals plight. As it so happened, Wyland was in town for an exhibition of his work at the Vancouver Aquarium. He was looking for walls to paint.

It didn't take long for Wyland and the mayor to meet one another and start collaborating on a Whaling Wall project for the city. Hogg arranged for the necessary permits and quickly generated a groundswell of community support, which, much to Wyland's delight, was a complete reversal of what he had encountered in Laguna Beach for his first Whaling Wall.

"It was very inspirational for me to receive warmth and encouragement from the people of White Rock," Wyland says. "They had such a tremendous appreciation for what I was doing, and I really wanted to give something back to them."

The 30'x70' mural was the artist's first international Whaling Wall. It depicts a mother gray whale, her calf and their male escort as they pass by White Rock on their annual migration from Baja, Mexico, to the Bering and Chukchi seas off Siberia. The 6,000-mile trip takes the whales six to eight weeks, at speeds of 160 kilometers (100 miles) per day.

During the painting of the wall, the city took care of Wyland's lodging and meals, and afterwards Mayor Hogg gave him the key to the city at the dedication ceremony. Because of his special relationship with the people of White Rock, Wyland returns often to visit this Whaling Wall, and also to see his good friends.

WHALING WALL 5
THE ORCAS OF PUGET SOUND

After completing the mural in White Rock, Wyland and his volunteer crew drove to Seattle, Washington, where he had been invited to paint a wall that was suspended over water on Seattle's Alaskan Way.

"The big challenge was getting the scaffolding across the water and over to the wall," the artist recalls. "Finally, this guy suggested we use some buoys and float the scaffolding over to the wall, and that's how we did it. A crew of volunteers then had to rappel down from the top and jump into the ice cold water to set it up."

Logistics aside, the mural was completed on the 50'x140' north wall of the Edgewater Inn showing an entire pod of orca whales, also known as killer whales, frolicking in the cool waters of Puget Sound.

Wyland remembers seeing numerous orcas swimming in the water nearby as he painted, and it occurred to him that perhaps the whales were watching him. "My idea was that maybe the orcas could see me painting a tribute to them, and that inspired me even more."

Unfortunately, the mural was later painted over by the new owners of the hotel, despite a furious protest from the community. "The mural is now extinct," Wyland laments. "Hopefully, that won't happen to the whales."

▲ 1984 **Whaling Wall V** — Seattle, Washington — 140 feet long x 50 feet high — Dedicated November 10, 1984 by Ivar Haglund, Seattle Port Manager

WHALING WALL 6
HAWAIIAN HUMPBACKS

Wyland was riding "The Bus" heading into Waikiki when he spotted in the distance exactly what he had been looking for — the perfect canvas on which to paint the humpback whales. As the bus drew closer, the artist got so excited that he pulled the stop cord as if there were an emergency and leaped off the vehicle as it pulled to a halt.

"I immediately saw a pod of humpbacks swimming across this huge wall," Wyland says. "At one end there was this tower section, and I envisioned a humpback jumping out of the water in a full breach."

Today, Wyland claims that when he finished painting the wall, it was not much different from this first picture he had formed in his mind. The majestic mural, 300 feet wide and 26 stories high, displayed life-size humpbacks cavorting across a clear blue ocean that looked like an extension of the real Hawaiian waters in the background. The painting also included a group of playful dolphins, false killer whales, green sea turtles and a variety of tropical fish. The 60-foot whale breeching up into the tower section looked so real that one expected to be splashed at any moment as the great beast cannoned back into the water.

The public's response to the Whaling Wall was no less phenomenal. Painted on the side of the Ilikai's marina condominium building, literally millions of wide-eyed tourists were met by the mural as they entered Waikiki. Those who watched Wyland use 900 gallons of paint to complete the half-acre wall found themselves being pulled into the energy and excitement generated by the project, with over 4,000 attending the dedication ceremony.

"At that time, the wall was next to Kaiser Hospital," Wyland says. "Some of the terminal cancer patients would watch from their windows as I painted the mural. I was told that a few of them stayed alive a little longer just so they could see the wall completed."

Alas, all was not completely well in Honolulu. The project was opposed by one group called The Outdoor Circle, and also a developer who wanted to build a luxury hotel next to the wall. The two groups dragged Wyland into court in a well-publicized lawsuit to stop the mural, but the artist won and was allowed to complete the work.

Development on the hotel continued, nonetheless. Most of the mural is now blocked from public view by the Hawaii Prince Hotel. Wyland says that by blocking out the wall, the developer has created an appropriate metaphor for what has happened to the whales — they are being closed out by man.

Painting "life-size" breaching humpbacks

Honolulu wall unpainted, Christmas day 1984

Dedication ceremony

Signing the mural, dedication day

Whaling Wall VI — Honolulu, Hawaii — 300 feet long x 26 stories high — Dedicated April 21, 1985 by Russ Francis, San Francisco 49ers

WHALING WALL 7
CALIFORNIA GRAY WHALES

WHALING WALL 8
ORCAS

After painting the internationally famous mural in Honolulu, Wyland returned to his goal of painting 100 Whaling Walls around the world. His next stop was Del Mar, California.

In trying to expose as many people as he could to his environmental message, he chose a 100′x16′ wall on Del Mar's Gem and Minerals Building, close to where an Amtrak train passed by every half hour. The mural shows gray whales swimming behind three playful dolphins.

"One of the most satisfying aspects of doing this wall was that Glenn Frey dedicated the wall and said some very nice things about the project," Wyland says, referring to the popular singer/songwriter and former Eagle. "Like me, he is from Michigan and makes one of his homes in Hawaii. He was a wonderful spokesperson for the mural."

The side of the Canada Life Insurance Company building in Vancouver, British Columbia, provided the surface for Wyland's eighth Whaling Wall. The artist says he wanted the mural to incorporate the environment of Vancouver and its local pods of orca whales swimming through the cool, flat waters.

"When you look at this mural from a distance, it actually blends into its surroundings," Wyland says. "I think the highest thing I can achieve in my work is to make the painting a natural extension of the beauty in the area."

The mural conveys the mystic haze that often hovers over the water near Vancouver in the mornings, and the group of orcas represents a local pod that frequents the region.

Canada Life, the company that sponsored Wyland during the project, was so taken with the mural that they renamed the building. It is now called The Wyland Building.

The Wyland building

▲ 1985 Whaling Wall VII — Del Mar, California — 100 feet long x 16 feet high — Dedicated July 6, 1985 by Glenn Frey, Eagles Singer/Songwriter

▲ **1985 Whaling Wall VIII** — Vancouver, British Columbia, Canada — 130 feet long x 70 feet high — Dedicated September 10, 1985 by Michael Harcourt, Mayor of Vancouver

WHALING WALL 9
FIRST VOYAGE

"First Voyage," which depicts the Polynesians' discovery of the Hawaiian Islands, was the first time Wyland incorporated humans into one of his Whaling Walls. The double-hulled canoes bearing the sturdy voyagers are escorted into the island by spirited dolphins who, perhaps, had never before seen humans and their sailing vessels.

"I had to do extensive research to make sure these canoes were accurate," Wyland explains. "I also had to be very accurate about the clothing that ancient Polynesians wore at the time. I really enjoy this aspect of my art, studying the subjects and trying to be as authentic as I can."

Magnum P.I. star John Hillerman dedicated this mural at the Polynesian Cultural Center.

WHALING WALL 10
MANATEES

Wyland's 10th Whaling Wall featured a different kind of marine mammal — the manatee. The artist was invited by Florida Governor Bob Graham and singer Jimmy Buffett, founder of the Save the Manatees Committee, to paint the endangered manatee at the Orlando International Airport.

Before he painted the mural, Wyland went diving at Blue Springs, Florida, and encountered several manatees up close. After spending four hours face-to-face with a group of the friendly creatures, he not only knew exactly how he would paint his mural, but he also was deeply affected by the experience.

"If you look at the painting, you'll see that I spent a lot of time with the eyes trying to capture the soul of this animal," Wyland explains. "I also painted some of the fungi on the mother's back, and you can see a few prop (propeller) marks as well. Manatees are often hit by sporting boats because they're slow-moving animals, and many of them have prop marks on their backs because they have trouble getting out of the way.

"Jimmy Buffett and the Save the Manatees group have done a tremendous job of raising awareness that these Florida waters are the only natural habitat for the manatees. People need to be more aware because these mammals are very fragile and sensitive to this ever-shrinking environment."

▲ 1986 Whaling Wall IX — Polynesian Cultural Center, Oahu, Hawaii — 130 feet long x 14 feet high — Dedicated February 4, 1986 by John Hillerman, Actor

…If we can save our oceans, we have a real chance of saving ourselves…

Painting life-size Manatees, Orlando International Airport

6 Whaling Wall X — Orlando, Florida — 14 feet long x 8 feet high — Dedicated 1986 by Jimmy Buffet, Singer/Songwriter

WHALING WALL 11
F I R S T   B O R N

When Wyland granted a request from Sea World in Orlando, Florida, to paint a mural of a baby orca whale and her mother, it was the first time the artist had done an actual portrait of his subjects.

The birth of Baby Shamu to her mother, Kandu, demonstrated that killer whales can be born and thrive under the care of man. This is a breakthrough contribution to the preservation of the orca for generations to come.

"The baby was one year old, and the unique thing was that we dedicated this mural at the exact time she had been born one year earlier," Wyland says. "This project was special for me in that I learned so much from studying and drawing these whales before I painted their portrait. The baby actually had some of the same markings the mother had and, to me, that's very special."

With orca, Taiji, Japan

▲ 1986 Whaling Wall XI — Sea World, Orlando, Florida — 30 feet long x 12 feet high - Dedicated September 26, 1986 by Bill Evans, Washington, D.C.

WHALING WALL 12
LAGUNA COAST

This mural was painted in 1987 on the side of Wyland's studio gallery in Laguna Beach. In the painting, a gray whale is "spyhopping" and looking at each and every person that drives past her on the way out of town.

"What I wanted to do is leave an impression about the Laguna coast and its fantastic marine life, including whales and the many different kinds of birds," Wyland says. "The wall is painted in such a way that you can't ignore it."

As for "politics and red tape," the likes of which Wyland experienced the first time he painted a wall in Laguna Beach, there weren't any this time. In fact, instead of controversy, the artist was greeted with a resounding proclamation from the city.

"I think the city is now beginning to realize the importance the murals have to the community," Wyland says.

▲ 1987 Whaling Wall XII — Laguna Beach, California — 20 feet long x 24 feet high - Dedicated February 2, 1987 by Darlene Wyland - Artist's Mom

WHALING WALL 14
SPERM WHALES

After the president of the Tokyo Bay Citizens Council saw Wyland's spectacular Whaling Wall VI in Hawaii, he invited the artist to come to Japan and paint a mural. Consisting mostly of local fishermen, residents and conservationists, the council was alarmed at the rate of development in Tokyo Bay, which they felt had already ruined much of the bay's fishing and marine ecosystem.

Wyland, on the other hand, had been looking for a way to make a statement in Japan. Preferring as always to remain apolitical about his commitment to the world's oceans, he wanted instead to use his art to expose the Japanese to the delicate beauty of whales and other creatures of the sea.

"I chose the sperm whale as my subject because they were being hunted off the coast of Japan at the time," Wyland explains. "I painted two of the whales on the seawall at Funabashi, and I wasn't sure how they would be received. But the Japanese people really appreciate art and artists, and their response was overwhelmingly positive. The mural was very beautiful and unique to them."

"I feel pretty confident in saying that this was probably the first time most Japanese had seen a whale, other than on a dinner plate."

Wyland felt he needed to make yet a bigger statement in Japan, and he took the opportunity during this first trip to visit the old whaling village of Taiji, where Japanese whaling had begun centuries earlier. He met the mayor of Taiji and talked to him about the possibility of one day replacing the country's whaling industry with whale-watching. The mayor appeared receptive, so the artist vowed he would return one day and paint a mural in the village. He even picked out a wall, located on the side of the Taiji whaling museum. Four years later, he fulfilled his vow.

Postcard

WHALING WALL 13
ORCAS A-5 POD

Wyland considers Whaling Wall XIII to be one of his most unique murals because it pictures an actual pod of orca whales that live off of Vancouver Island. This particular pod contains 13 orcas known as the "A-5 Pod." The dominant male in the group, "A-5," has a large, distinctive six-foot dorsal fin with a nick.

Each member of the pod was painted in its true size with its individual features. The mother of the baby orca in the lower left corner of the mural, for instance, is named "Sharky" because her dorsal fin looks like that of a shark.

"I worked with the top scientists in the world on this project — Mike Bigg, Graham Ellis and John Ford," Wyland says. "Mike Bigg is noted as the top orca researcher in the world, and he has been studying these whales and these waters for 30 years. I actually had Mike get up on the scaffolding with me with a piece of chalk and a photograph of each of the whales to help me correct the anatomy on each whale."

Wyland was particularly pleased that his friend, artist, Robert Bateman, who is considered by many to be the world's leading wildlife artist, flew in from his nearby home on Salt Spring Island to dedicate the wall to the city of Victoria. During the ceremony, Bateman looked up and noticed a bald eagle in the painting and said jokingly, "Wyland, I thought we had an agreement — you we going to paint below the ocean, and I was going to paint above think you're starting to take over."

Wyland included the bald eagle at the request of a native Indian who showed him one of the great birds pictured on a postcard and asked him if he would consider adding it to the mu Wyland took the man up on the scaffolding and painted it in for a moment the artist still recalls with great pride.

▲ 1987 Whaling Wall XIV — Funabashi, Japan — 140 feet long x 18 feet high — Dedicated October 14, 1987 by Dr. Goro Tomeraga, Professor Emeritus, and Mr. Ono

1987 Whaling Wall XIII — Victoria, British Columbia, Canada — 130 feet long x 4 stories high — Dedicated June 20, 1987 In memory of Robin Morton, dedicated by Robert Bateman

View across the street, Victoria, B.C.

Robert Bateman dedicating mural

Mike Bigg explaining orca anatomy

WHALING WALL 15
DOLPHINS OFF MAKAPUU POINT

When Wyland climbed up on his scaffolding to paint Whaling Wall XV at Oahu's Sea Life Park, he had planned to paint Pacific bottlenose dolphins only. But, when he turned around and looked back at the sea, he saw a breathtaking view of the beautiful turquoise and azure waters off Makapuu Point, and he changed his mind.

The mural at the popular park now bears the life-size bottlenose dolphins Wyland had wanted to paint, but it also shows the stunning landmark of Makapuu Point in the backgound. "I have a special love for Sea Life Park and this area because this is where I conducted much of my research on dolphins and other sea creatures," the artist says.

Singer/songwriter Henry Kapono, a good friend of Wyland's, dedicated the wall and then gave a concert at the park in honor of the mural. The singer has since written a special song for his friend called "Wyland's Song."

WHALING WALL 16
ORCAS OFF POINT LOMA

An indoor swimming pool in Mission Beach, California, would provide the stage for Wyland's next mural. Appropriately called "The Plunge," the huge pool had served local residents in the area since the '20s. Having been recently restored, the owners of the pool wanted Wyland to paint the large wall that overlooks the water, which, at one time, had actually borne another mural.

Wyland saw this project as an excellent opportunity to paint the orca whales that frequented the waters off Point Loma. San Diego researchers took him out in a boat and showed him a local pod they had been studying, and soon thereafter, this group of life-size orcas was giving the word "plunge" new meaning as they loomed high above the old swimming pool.

"Most people don't realize that orcas live off of the California Coast," Wyland points out. "In fact, orcas live in almost all of the oceans on earth. I hope people will begin to realize just how precious they are and that they existed on this planet long before man claimed it for his own."

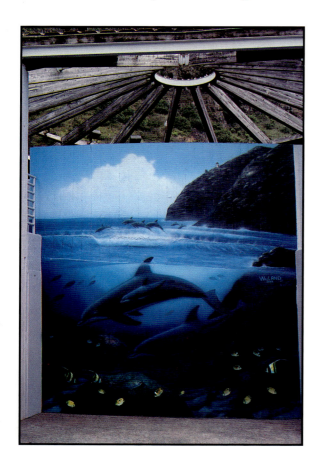

▲ 1988 Whaling Wall XV — Sea Life Park, Oahu, Hawaii — 24 feet long x 30 feet high — Dedicated by Henry Kapono, Singer/Songwriter

Painting orcas, San Diego, CA

1989 Whaling Wall XVI — The Plunge, Mission Beach, San Diego, California — 140 feet long x 40 feet high — Dedicated June 29, 1989 by Bob Gault, President of Sea World

WHALING WALL 17
BOTTLENOSE DOLPHINS

WHALING WALL
SPERM WHALES OFF THE MEDITERRANE

Wyland made his second trip to Japan when he was asked to paint a mural at Sinjiku Station for "24-Hour Television." Essentially, it was a day-long telethon to raise money to help the planet, and Wyland was to complete one of his Whaling Walls within the 24-hour marathon.

"I painted this mural outside, in front of literally hundreds of thousands of Japanese citizens," Wyland recalls. "It was carried live over national television, and the message was carried throughout Japan."

The painting depicts two bottlenose dolphins cavorting through the Pacific. Over $70 million were raised during the telethon to fund conservation efforts throughout Japan. Only today have the Japanese begun to realize the impact of over-fishing and misuse of our natural resources. As a result, environmental groups are beginning to emerge within Japan.

Wyland's goal of painting 100 murals throughout the world took h to Europe, where he painted an 11-st building in Nice, France. The paintir portrays a mother sperm whale and her baby diving through the clear blue waters of the Mediterranean.

Above the ocean looms the French Riviera, with dolphins surfaci "Today, the Mediterranean is dying due to pollution and other environmental problems," Wyland says. "T mural is an international symbol to bring attention to these fragile wat and to educate the public."

"A unique thing happened as a result of the building's design," he continues. "Two windows appeared inside the mother and baby whale. I felt the urge to go inside the building and experience being inside a whale like Jonah. To say the least, I received a lot of strange looks as people drove past their cars."

Sumo wrestler Konishiki

Nice, France mural

▲ **Whaling Wall XVII** — Osaka, Japan — 20 feet long x 30 feet high - Dedicated August 27, 1989 by Mr. Toshita and Kent Fabulous. Wall was painted for a 24-hr. Telethon in Japan

Whaling Wall XVIII — Nice, France — 42 feet long x 120 feet high — Dedicated October, 1989 by French Government Official

WHALING WALL 19
FORBIDDEN REEF

Returning from Europe, Wyland began painting two murals for Sea World in San Diego. Forbidden Reef features marine life of Southern California, such as bat rays, eels, garibaldi and other fish of the Pacific.

The exhibit begins with a journey into the ocean realm leading into caverns of natural habitats for these marine creatures.

"Painting the mural was the easy part, and all that was left was to sign my name," Wyland recalls. "I was joking with the media and stated, 'I hope I spelled my name right.' Someone from the audience pointed out that I had, in fact, left out a letter. All I can say is that I tried to buy all the film that was shot that day."

I hope I spell my name right

Oops!

Artists aren't known for their spelling

▲ 1990 Whaling Wall XIX — Sea World, San Diego, California — 90 feet long x 14 feet high — Dedicated July 9, 1990 by Michael Peak, Author

WHALING WALL 20
GRAY WHALE MIGRATION

"If I was to build a perfect wall for one of my murals, it would be just like the one I painted at Sea World," Wyland says. "The wall was long enough to feature three gray whales and literally curved around the viewer, creating a three-dimensional quality."

Wyland's 20th Whaling Wall was completed in front of 30,000 people a day during the summer of 1990. The wall has become a favorite photo location for the 4 million who visit Sea World each year.

Touching friendly gray whales — Mexico

1990 Whaling Wall XX — Sea World, San Diego, California — 80 feet long x 15 feet high — Dedicated July 9, 1990 by Bob Gault, President of Sea World

WHALING WALL 21
WASHINGTON ORCAS

During the Goodwill Games in the summer of 1990, Wyland traveled to Washington to complete Whaling Wall XXI. He began by painting Mount Rainier and the Pacific's cool waters, home to many pods of killer whales.

"I wanted to portray a family of orcas travelling the waters off the Washington Coast," explains the artist. "A mother orca teaches her baby to breach as a bald eagle soars by, a scene very familiar to local residents."

As he neared completion of the mural, it occurred to Wyland that the Goodwill Games should thereafter be called the "Goodwhale Games."

WHALING WALL 22
ORCA HEAVEN

"This by far is my most unique mural in that it's the first one I painted on a ceiling," says Wyland. "When I first saw this ceiling, I had an immediate vision of orcas swimming overhead. And I wanted to give the illusion of being underwater looking up at the surface of the ocean as the powerful orcas swam above."

The background colors developed naturally until the artist began painting the first whale. Having trouble with the perspective, Wyland's brother, Bill, suggested that he tape a piece of chalk onto a yardstick and lay on his back to sketch in the whale.

"At first, I resisted," Wyland explains. "But, finally, I decided to try this technique and found it to be the solution to the problem. From there, it was simply a matter of painting in the chalk drawing. I was able to complete the ceiling in only three days."

▲ 1990 Whaling Wall XXI — Tacoma, Washington — 120 feet long x 45 feet high — Dedicated July, 1990 by Tacoma Mayor, Karen Vialle

▲ 1990 Whaling Wall XXII — Yamagata, Japan (Ceiling) — 145 feet long x 45 feet high — Dedicated 1990 by Mr. Kawada, President, Sun Marina Corporation

WHALING WALL 23
BUNDABERG HUMPBACK FAMILY

After completing the ceiling mural in Yamagata, Japan, Wyland boarded a plane to begin painting his first mural in the Southern Hemisphere. The City of Bundaberg, Australia, rolled out the red carpet for Wyland and crew as he began painting a huge building in the center of the City.

Wyland spent a lot of time diving the Great Barrier Reef in preparation for the mural. Humpback whales frequent these waters along with loggerhead turtles and other diverse marine life. Upon completing the mural, the city hosted the artist in a lighting ceremony that was attended by over 5,000 people.

"It was the warmest reception I have ever received," he says. "It seemed the entire community became involved in this project, and I was invited to paint a second mural in Australia at the Sydney Aquarium."

WHALING WALL 24
HUMPBACK AND CALF

The Sydney Aquarium in Darling Harbor hosted Wyland's second mural in Australia. Upon entering the famous aquarium, visitors encountered for the first time a life-size portrait of humpback whales.

"This painting represents my most realistic portrayal of a mother humpback with her baby swimming through a cathedral of light," Wyland says.

Darling Harbor — one of Sydney's most populated areas — is visited annually by millions of international travelers as well as local citizens. As a result, the mural offers a far-reaching message about the ocean's gentle giants.

▲ 1990 Whaling Wall XXIII — Bundaberg, Australia — 125 feet long x 95 feet high — Dedicated September 28, 1990 by John Nielsen

...Whales swim through a cathedral of light pyramiding through the deep blue ocean, creating a spiritual sensation unequalled...

▲ 1990 Whaling Wall XXIV — Sydney Aquarium, Sydney, Australia — 90 feet long x 35 feet high — Dedicated September 28, 1990 by Jim Longley, Parliament, New South Wales

WHALING WALL 25
HUMPBACKS

At his 15-year high school reunion, Wyland was asked by his former high school principal, Jim McCann, to paint a mural for his Alma Mater. Wyland agreed. After presentations to the students of Lamphere High School and Page Junior High School, Wyland and a group of art students began painting Whaling Wall XXV.

Wyland taught his mural technique to the students as they completed the painting on a large wall overlooking the school's swimming pool. The mural was finished in an 18-hour marathon, attended by hundreds of Wyland's former classmates and teachers, as well as his dad.

"It felt great to give something back to my school and share my work with the young artists," Wyland says proudly. An art scholarship in his name was established to support and encourage aspiring young artists.

WHALING WALL 27
MINKE WHALE

A second mural in Marathon in the Florida Keys was completed at the Natural History Museum in only three hours. The painting features a minke whale with a green sea turtle and a large manta ray.

"The mural reveals windows into the ocean allowing the viewer to encounter these fascinating creatures," says Wyland. "The museum has many classrooms for students, and this mural provides them with a firsthand look at these animals in their true size."

▲ 1990 Whaling Wall XXV — Lamphere High School, Detroit, Michigan — 110 feet long x 15 feet high - Dedicated October 31, 1990 by James McCann, Principal

▲ Whaling Wall XXVII — Museum of Natural History — Marathon Keys, Florida — 40 feet long x 8 feet high Dedicated October 30, 1990 by Mandy Rodriquez, Dolphin Research Center

WHALING WALL 26
SPERM WHALES AND FLORIDA REEF

Dolphin Research Center director and longtime friend Mandy Rodriquez secured two wall locations in the Florida Keys for Wyland murals. By far the largest wall in the area was on the K-Mart building fronting the A1A Highway.

"I wanted to showcase the variety of sealife found in the Florida Keys, and this wall was ideal for that purpose," Wyland says. "Having spent years diving in the area, I was anxious to paint the many living reefs and animals that inhabit these waters."

"This sensitive ecosystem is being destroyed by man's misuse and over-development, and I wanted to bring attention to this critical situation. I hope in some small way the mural will be a reminder to all who view it that we must save our living reefs."

Dedication Florida Keys mural

aling Wall XXVI — Marathon Keys, Florida — 140 feet long x 20 feet high — Dedicated October 30, 1990 by Marathon Keys former mayor

WHALING WALL 28
A TIME FOR CONSERVATION

Again feeling the need to express his art, Wyland completed two murals in Kapaa, Kauai. The first was a clock tower and, as he began painting around the 360-degree tower, a message rang out loud and clear to him: "It's time for conservation."

As a humpback whale breached across the rugged Na Pali coast, the painting came alive. "As I stood on the scaffolding painting this great whale, I realized how magnificent these creatures are," Wyland recalls. "The only thing that compares to painting the animal life-size would be witnessing the living whale clearing its 40 tons out of the ocean. You could almost feel the salt spray as the mural was completed." This is the first time I've used the Hawaiian landscape in one of my Whaling Walls."

WHALING WALL 29
HUMPBACKS OFF THE NA PALI COAST

After completing the clock mural in Kapaa, Kauai, Wyland painted a companion mural nearby. The painting depicts the long, rugged Na Pali coast and offers a view of the shore from above and below the ocean.

Featured in the mural are a life-size green sea turtle and Wyland's first Hawaiian monk seal, which is indigenous to the waters of Kauai.

"The monk seal is very endangered, and I wanted to bring some attention to this incredible native of the islands," says Wyland. "The mural seems to blend into the natural environment as the clouds drift across the sky and into the painting, becoming one with the land."

Watching Whales

▲ Whaling Wall XXVIII — Kauai Village, Kauai, Hawaii — 44 feet high walls, 360 degree mural on clock tower — Dedicated January 8, 1991 By Ron Kouchi, County Council Chairman

▲ **Whaling Wall XXIX** — Kauai, Hawaii — 150 feet long ∷ 24 feet high — Dedicated January 8, 1991 By Peter Alevizos, Kauai Village President

Maui Humpback Breaching, painting

WHALING WALL 30
MAUI HUMPBACK BREACHING

"When I moved to Lahaina, Maui, to study the humpback whales, I read about Lahaina's whaling days and the waters off of Maui that were breeding grounds of the humpbacks. I rented a small studio on Front Street in downtown Lahaina. Each day I'd try to learn about the history . . . I wanted to paint a realistic depiction of Lahaina's whaling past and present.

As soon as I arrived, I noticed a wall rising from the seawall on Front Street. The wall offered me the perfect opportunity to paint a life-size humpback. I did a rendering of what the wall would look like completed and approached the Lahaina Restoration Society with my plans.

To make a long story short, the mural was rejected. After nine years, I decided it was time for conservation, and the heck with politics. At 3 a.m. on a Friday morning, myself and a volunteer crew assembled scaffolding at the base of the wall and began painting. It was dark, and I could barely see the wall, but I had painted the mural in my mind's eye so many times that I could have done it blindfolded. When the sun came up, I was amazed at the detail and beauty of the painting that I had wanted to paint for so many years.

I knew that I would be subjected to substantial opposition from the 'Lahaina Hysterical Society,' but felt in my heart that the vast majority of people supported our efforts to paint the first Whaling Wall in Lahaina. At a special dedication ceremony and blessing, I was asked how long the mural took to paint. I can honestly say nine years and two days. Today the mural is endangered as are the humpbacks themselves."

Blank sea wall, Laihaina, Maui

Whales eye view of Lahaina wall

naling Wall XXX — Lahaina, Maui, Hawaii — 26 feet long × 30 feet high - Dedicated January 21, 1991 by John Pitre and Jerry Lopez

WHALING WALL 31
GRAY WHALE MIGRATION

The city of Redondo Beach, California, asked Wyland to paint a giant mural on the side of the Southern California Edison Power Plant. The massive wall was an industrial eyesore in the community, and the Chamber of Commerce, along with numerous city officials, invited Wyland to Redondo Beach to see it.

"This, by far, was the ugliest wall I had ever seen," Wyland recalls. "But at the same time, I was awed by its sheer size and potential for a Whaling Wall. I immediately envisioned an entire pod of gray whales migrating across the wall."

Wyland began painting the mural in June of 1991. The city felt it would take 12 months to complete the mural, but Wyland insisted he could complete it in 12 days. After spraying over 3,000 gallons of paint and covering nearly an acre and a half, the 622-foot-long by 10-story-high wall was completed in a record 11 days.

Along with nine life-size gray whales, Wyland painted his first blue whale, over 100 feet long, accompanied by Pacific bottlenose dolphins and giant, 70 foot high kelp forests reaching the surface of the ocean.

The mural, considered the largest of its kind in the United States, can be seen from Catalina Island, 26 miles away.

"Probably the most unusual thing about this mural is the unique Halogen lighting that Southern California Edison provided to enhance its beauty at night," Wyland says. "Now the mural can be enjoyed 24 hours a day."

▲ **Whaling Wall XXXI** — Redondo Beach, Califonia — 622 feet long x 100 feet high (1-1/4 acre) — Dedicated June 24, 1991 by John Bryson, CEO, Southern California Edison

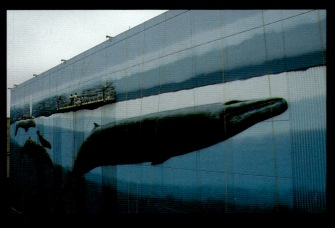

JUNE 3, 1991

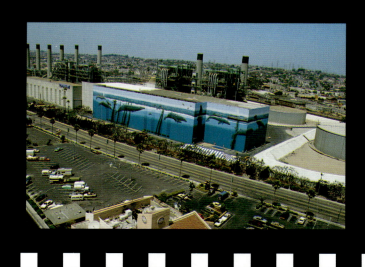

JUNE 14, 1991 — 11 DAYS LATER

WHALING WALL 32
RIGHT WHALES

Wyland first visited Taiji in 1987, after completing his first mural in Japan in Funabashi. Four years later, in August 1991, he fulfilled a dream by painting an historic mural on the exterior of Taiji's whaling museum. Japanese whaling started in Taiji in 1606 when the first right whale was harpooned. Whalers called them "right whales" because they were the only large whales that floated after they were killed.

Right whales were the symbol of Taiji whaling, and after much thought and conversation by the people of Taiji, Wyland decided to paint a life-size mother right whale and her baby.

"I wanted to paint the living whales and show the people of Taiji the beauty of these gentle giants," Wyland says. "I felt if I could paint the right whales swimming free in their own environment, the Japanese and many visitors to this coastal community would see what I see when I look at whales."

The artist was assisted by one of the Japanese whalers who provided photos and books of right whales and guided Wyland's hand from across the street, helping with the proportion and anatomy of each whale. When it was completed, the whaler commented on the beauty of the whales' eyes.

"I hope that this mural will begin a new understanding of how we view God's greatest creatures," Wyland concludes.

Dedication at Taiji whaling wall, Japan

Whaling Wall XXXII — Taiji Whaling Museum, Taiji, Japan — 35' high x 100' long — Dedicated August 29, 1991 by Taiji Town Mayor

Artist at dedication with Taiji mayor and city officials

WHALING WALL 33
PLANET OCEAN

May 3, 1992 Wyland completed painting the largest mural in the world at the Long Beach Convention Center on the Long Beach Arena.

Entitled "Planet Ocean," it was completed in only 6 weeks and required 7,000 gallons of paint. "This mural, Whaling Wall XXXIII, to me is a symbol of our environmental times and carries a message that in order to save the whales, we must first save our "Planet Ocean."

Featuring marine life indigenous to Southern California, the finished mural included a pod of gray whales, orca whales, blue whales, pilot whales, pacific bottlenose dolphins California sea lions, sharks, garabaldi and a variety of other fish. Everything in the mural is painted life-size. The mural itself is over ten stories high and 1,225 feet in diameter (almost 3 acres) the entire 360 degree surface of the Long Beach Arena. Monday, May 4, 1992, the Guinness World Book of Records certified Wyland's mural as the largest ever created.

The dedication ceremony was attended by Team Wyland's 200 volunteers and thousands of supporters and brought Wyland closer to realizing his goal of 100 walls by the year 2011.

..."Its No Big Thing"... WyLAND

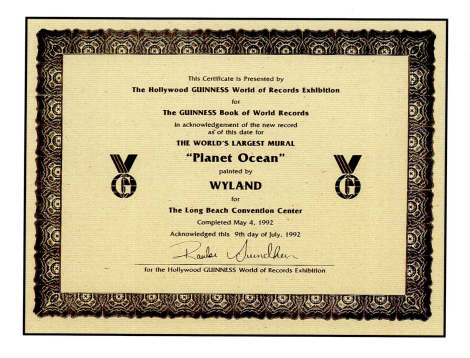

Whaling Wall XXXIII — Long Beach, California — 1,270 Diameter x 110 Feet High (Guiness Book of World Record — Dedicated July 9, 1992 by Chris Robinson Actor

WHALING WALL 34
OCEAN BIOSPHERE

Biosphere 2 invited Wyland to paint one of his Whaling Walls at their site in Oracle, Arizona. After nearly a year of preparation, the artist and his crew arrived to an enthusiastic reception by the entire staff and the six Biospherians.

Several months earlier, Wyland went to the Orange County Marine Institute to participate in a satellite teleconference call with ocean scientist Abigail Alling, who was at the Biosphere 2. They were finally ready to meet in person and discuss the theme of Wyland's latest effort.

Biosphere 2 had an ocean and living reef inside. When Abigail and the research team collected the various coral and fish, they were visited by a family of Pacific bottlenose dolphins. "Storytelling sometimes plays a big part in the painting of my murals, and I felt that re-creating the spirit of the special visit by the dolphins would be most appropriate."

The Biospherians were able to view the entire mural start-to-finish from a live video monitor. "It was a great experience for me when Lloyd Bridges and his son, Beau, came by and painted some fish on the mural," Wyland recalls.

"Lloyd couldn't help painting "Sea Hunt Lives" on my pants. Owner Ed Bass also painted, saying later it was the most fun he'd had since the Biosphere opened."

WHALING WALL 35
ORCAS OFF THE OREGON COAST

Wyland painted his first Oregon Whaling Wall in downtown Portland. The large mural captures the unique beauty of a pod of orca whales off the beautiful coast of Oregon.

"I've spent a lot of time over the past 15 years enjoying Oregon's Pacific coast, and I wanted to share that unique beauty with the many visitors and residents of Portland," Wyland says.

The mayor of Portland proclaimed May 5 "Wyland Day" as the artist began to cover the 120-foot-long, 60-foot-high wall with masses of Northwest colors. Soon the picturesque coastline began to appear, followed by a calm Pacific Ocean. One by one, Wyland painted each orca, creating an entire pod of five whales.

The official dedication was attended by thousands of enthusiastic Oregonians, who now can claim the Portland Whaling Wall as their own.

With Biospherians

Whaling Wall XXXIV — Tuscon, Arizona — 110 feet long x 30 feet high — Dedicated April 18, 1993 by Lloyd Bridges

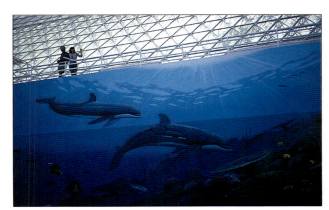
Biosphere above and below

Crowd for official dedication, Portland

Detail Portland mural

Completed mural

▲ **Whaling Wall XXXV** — Portland, Oregon — 120 feet long x 60 feet high — Dedicated May 9, 1993 by Darlene Wyland

V
PAINTING THE LARGEST MURAL IN THE WORLD

...There's no rest when you're on planetary duty...

▲ Finishing Whaling Wall 33, "Planet Ocean" — Long Beach, CA 1992

Blank wall - oil drum or minimalist architecture?

First day chaos

Priming and sealing the wall

I received a phone call one day at my Hawaii studio inviting me to fly to California and discuss the possibility of painting a Whaling Wall in Long Beach. The idea was for me to have lunch with the mayor, city planner and other prominent members of the community on the Queen Mary, the famous cruise vessel that had adopted Long Beach as its home port. Flattered and curious, I accepted and ate a wonderful lunch with about 40 Long Beach city officials. After we ate, they took me topside to look at the City of Long Beach from one of the higher decks of the Queen Mary. The vantage point had been carefully selected so that we were looking over what I would later find out was the Long Beach Sports Arena and Convention Center.

As I looked out the window, I saw this giant, round cylinder. It was huge, 110 feet high and 1,225 feet in circumference. I immediately commented, "There's a perfect wall right there."

"You got it!" they said. This was the wall they wanted me to paint; it was already planned. I asked them where we were on approval to paint the center. They told me I had just had lunch with everyone who was needed to grant permission. All I had to do was say "yes," and tell them what I needed.

I was pretty confident I could paint it, but I would need a tremendous amount of support from the City and enough time, materials and volunteers. As I looked at the wall, I began to envision a theme of Southern California marine life, depicting the many whales, dolphins and other indigenous sea life.

I decided I would do it, and we scheduled to paint the wall in the spring, after I returned from spending the winter at my home in Hawaii. Not long

Color Plan

after I returned to Oahu, however, the whole thing erupted into a major controversy. I had felt from the beginning something was wrong; it all sounded too good to be true. It seems the City kind of back-doored the project and didn't involve all segments of the Long Beach community. The Art Association of Long Beach was very upset that they'd been passed over without being consulted and had incited the media to join them in calling foul. A circus of propaganda and misinformation swept through Long Beach.

Then the City informed me they couldn't get any funding. It was the opposite of what I had been told. They said they'd finance the project, donate the paint and scaffolding and get as many volunteers as I needed. Now they were saying they weren't even going to be able to donate one dollar. The entire financial burden was unexpectedly hoisted onto my shoulders. Not only would I have to paint the largest mural in the world, I would have to supply the paint, the scaffolding, all supplies, everything.

I decided the wall was still worth doing, though. Sinclair Paint sold me the paint for cost, which ended up costing over $50,000 out of my pocket. The wall first had to be washed and prepared, another $30,000. And the other costs, tools and scaffolding, meant another $50,000. By the time all was said and done, it cost me nearly $200,000 of my own money to do this mural. Plus, I had blocked out eight weeks for the project, which kept me from painting in the studio, costing me even more. Had it not been for the success I was enjoying as a fine artist, there was no way I would have been able to do this mural.

The first thing my team had to do was pressure-wash the wall with high-powered water. That was quite a job because they had to go up on the scaffolding and blow off some of the old paint. Then they had to tape up all of the windows, which took close to a month. I knew going in it was going to be quite an effort, and I was more than right. Fortunately, our labor pool grew to 200 volunteers, from the vice-mayor to street people to everyone in between. Eventually, we managed to get organized with a paint crew, an office crew, an office Mom, a scaffolding crew and an equipment crew. The scope of this project was unequaled by any I'd ever known, except perhaps Cristo's running fence.

The paint was brought in by the semi-truckloads — 7,000 gallons, enough to fill several storage rooms. I was wondering how I'd get most of it up on that wall. It was really intimidating, and the more I looked at the wall, the more I questioned whether I could actually achieve this. Roy, though, was con-

Beginning giant bands of color

First whales swim up on the wall

Finished mural - 6 weeks and 7,000 gallons of paint later

Long Beach fire department rescue

Climbing down 100' fireladder

stantly at my side and was teaming up with other professional painters to prepare the wall with a good coat of epoxy primer. When this was done and the primer dried, Roy and I began painting massive bands of background color on the wall. There were probably 12 different bands of color that had to be applied around the entire circumference of the wall — all 1,225 feet.

It took a lot of planning and organizing. But most of all, it was just plain old-fashioned hard work. By the second day I couldn't even lift my arm up I had sprayed so many gallons of paint. It was unbelievably physical. Eventually we had painted enough sections that I could start painting the marine life. When I got that first whale on the wall, it seemed like the spirit of the entire city changed overnight. Even the media began writing positive stories. Reporters and cameramen started coming down to the site and seeing for themselves what a tremendous effort it really was, not only by me, but by the volunteers.

About one week into the mural, I had painted several whales, and we were getting a lot of attention. The following weekend the Long Beach Grand Prix was scheduled to start, and the race route would go all the way around the mural site. Over 200,000 people were expected to attend the event, which meant they would all be able to see the Whaling Wall. The crew from ABC's *Wide World of Sports* came up and asked me if they could do a segment on my work. "Absolutely," I told them, and right in the middle of the Grand Prix telecast they cut to a feature on my work, with highlights of me painting the mural.

To me, this was an unlikely but effective vehicle to promote whale conservation. There were a lot of people sitting there watching the Grand Prix. I was intrigued by this chance to inspire them, even if they happened to be sitting in their living rooms watching the race on TV.

I completed a California gray whale section — an entire life-size pod migrating. Then, I finished a family of blue whales — a mother, her calf and their escort. I also painted myself in the mural, which was the first time I'd done that. The idea wasn't just to paint myself, but to show a diver so people could see how large these creatures are.

Afterward, I went on to paint a pod of orca whales. All of these whales are indigenous to waters off Southern California. About midway through the mural, we started calling it *Planet Ocean*, which seemed to be the perfect title because it signified how important the ocean is to the earth.

At some point, I had hoped to give everyone a

day off. But I knew that to finish we would have to paint continuously. We started painting at 7:00 or 8:00 in the morning and continued until 6:00 or 7:00 that night, seven days a week. As I painted all the way around the arena, I kept looking around the curve in the wall for the place I had started. Six weeks later I saw the other end. The curvature of the wall was interesting in that it presented a unique challenge. If I was painting a blue whale, I would be painting the body and not be able to see the head or tail. I had to envision the entire whale in my mind's eye. It was like an out-of-body experience — while my body was up on the scaffolding, my mind's eye was on the ground looking at the entire wall. I liked the way everything turned out, though. The roundness gave the mural more of a three-dimensional quality, a never-ending mural.

It was not all smooth sailing, however. In the fifth week, news of the Rodney King verdict suddenly invaded every television screen in America. As soon as the verdict came down, the riots started and immediately a guy on a motorcycle was murdered very near the wall. As I painted on toward the end of that day, there were many fires and gun shots near the Convention Center. We could see the fires clearly from the scaffolding, and there were bullets literally flying over our heads. To say it was unnerving would be an understatement. It was downright scary.

I finished the wall the night the riots ended. We had a special dedication ceremony and my friend, actor Chris Robinson, dedicated the mural along with Vice Mayor Jeff Kellogg, who, with his assistant, Linda Pope, had supported me and worked so hard on the project. The mural was, for me, my greatest challenge. It was not only the largest, but it required the most perseverance and stamina. It took everything I had to complete this wall, but it was definitely worth it. On the day of the dedication, the head of the Guinness Book of World Records presented me with a certificate, certifying that it was the largest mural ever painted.

I remember looking at the wall when it was finished from my hotel room at the Sheraton across the street. I could see the giant white circular roof of the sports arena. Ever since, I've had thoughts of going back and breaking my own world's record and adding to that mural. With seven-eighths of the earth covered by water, the earth is, by any definition, a water planet. I'd like to illustrate this by painting the top of *Planet Ocean* with a view from space, tying it into the sides, making it an even larger mural.

Whew

After graduating from college, I conducted some scientific research and therefore could have been considered a scientist. My specialty was the study of birds of prey; falcons, hawks, owls and eagles. But, when I first saw whales in the wild, I knew that they and the elephant had to be the ultimate forms of natures's designs here on earth. I had worked with elephants in Africa, but had not had an opportunity to observe their marine counterpart, humpback whales, exploding to the surface from beneath a school of herring. After choreographing a behavior called lunge feeding, they got my attention. Especially whales with their 14 foot mouths wide open, all coming up at once singing and talking to each other on the way up to spring the trap in unison.

I had already realized that research and science is great and important, but the challenge today is to make people care; affect public attitudes so voters in turn can affect government policy. We have already destroyed wildlife and habitat at a frightening rate. Science hasn't stopped the destruction. There needs to be a new emphasis placed on affecting peoples ability to be concerned and to care deeply. Wyland's whales, large and powerful enough to demand public attention were a sign to me that someone else felt the same way. Here was a monument as large as a building that had feeling and depth so that I felt the ocean was flooding the city, bringing the beauty and serenity of nature to the forefront of busy people's urban lives. The murals demanded attention and joined other priorities as being important to our lives. Great, I thought. It sure beats a stuffed carcass or plaster replica in a crowded museum. I was particularly impressed with the feeling of totality one gets from the painting. Although it is impossible for any artist to depict the complete diversity of ocean ecosystems, Wyland comes close by creating a feeling of the mystery of the sea with a few sprays of color and movement.

I began hearing about Wyland for a while before I met him at Art Expo in Los Angeles where my wife, Betsy, was showing her paintings of elephants. He was as enthusiastic about whales as Betsy and I were about elephants. I could tell immediately that this person not only cared about whales, but also why the existence of whales and all forms of life are important to us and our children.

I still don't know Wyland as well as I would like. When he came to New York and asked me to help dedicate his whale wall there and allowed me to sign my name next to his, I realized that here is a man who has a mission and lets nothing get in the way of completing this task. Taking on New York City, with its hundreds of committees, boards and generally negative regulation-oriented bureaucracies, shows that he knew a lot more than just how to spray paint. Greeting a person known as being more of a crocodile wrestler than a whale expert to brave 42nd Street and the jungle of the Port Authority definitely shows imagination.

Little did he know that I would have traveled around the world with him, watching him paint whales and signing walls if it would help focus human's attention of the saving of the ocean habitat. It is the ocean that controls our destiny. Besides, I once saw a humpback whale burst out of a lagoon, look at me and trumpet a noise that sounded like an elephant.

We are all somehow connected, it seems, and have to stick together if this world is to continue to provide fun, excitement, amazement and adventure in the outdoors. That to me is essential to the quality of life that, once you've got, assures a feeling of enjoyment that can't be taken away.

Wyland radiates that joy, and it's infectious! He must have looked into the eye of a whale too. Wyland's whales in cities will do more to save them and their ocean habitat than spending another 20 years studying their feeding habits and social life. Wyland's murals will make people care!

Jim Fowler

VI
17 MURALS, 17 CITIES, 17 WEEKS

...The time to rest is in the grave...

▲ New landmark Whaling Wall 50, downtown Atlanta, GA 1993

Traveling through Boston

Briefing the crew, Portland, ME

Drying the steel wall, Portland

Painting Portland wall

Dedication day crowds, Portland, ME

The first time I talked about doing a series of Whaling Walls along the Atlantic Seaboard was in 1988 when I was in Deer Island, Maine, visiting a friend of mine, singer/songwriter Dan Fogelberg. I'd heard about a whale researcher at the College of the Atlantic named Steven Katona and went to visit him.

We hit if off immediately, talking at length about how science and art have always been somewhat at odds with one another. We decided that my murals, which depict anatomically correct life-size whales and marine life, represent an opportunity for science and art to work together to accomplish something really important.

It made sense. I'd always wanted to paint the Atlantic Ocean and its vast array of marine life. Plus, I was starting to receive more and more requests from various cities on the East Coast to paint Whaling Walls. Five years later, I was sitting in my living room in Hawaii with my assistant, Angela Eaton, and Sondra and Jim Augenstein, my special events coordinators. "Why don't we just do it?," I said. "We can make one trip and do them all — just get it over with."

First, we needed money. And we needed donors for our paint and other materials. The task was so formidable I didn't know if we could get it all together before the tour was scheduled to start. However, we received an overwhelming response from all the cities we contacted, and that encouraged us to go for it.

Fortunately, we had Sondra to set this tour up and remove all the obstacles we might encounter. Normally, it would take over a year or more to gain approval to paint a mural in some of these cities, but Sondra blasted through the red tape and politics in a matter of months. In addition, we contacted every single person we knew to assist with the project. And they responded beyond our expectations.

As a precursor to this marathon, we embarked on a press tour that was pretty phenomenal in itself. We visited all 17 cities in 14 days. It was like a rock tour. In most of the cities, I'd only have a few hours to spend. And, in a few of them, they had yet to find a wall. In Rhode Island, the city officials hadn't found a site so I took them out on the freeway and found a wall for them.

I did a large art show in San Diego just before we were to start the tour, and thousands of people attended to send us off. Earlier that afternoon, I'd painted a mural depicting humpback whales on the side of a brand-new, 50-foot trailer donated by National Van Lines. I loved the idea of this mural traveling all over the country, exposing as many people as we could to the beauty of these whales. It was like I was taking the creatures on the road, literally.

At the end of May, we arrived in Portland, Maine ready to whale on the first of 17 murals, in 17 cities, in 17 weeks. The media came out in droves. The press coverage — local, national and international — was phenomenal during the entire tour. But we had a little delay in Portland. We had to wait around under our press tents as a rainstorm had its way with the city. By the afternoon, I got sick of waiting and ran out onto the pier and did a no-rain dance. I know this is going to sound crazy — but after about 15 minutes, the rain stopped. Call it luck, divine intervention or just a simple break in the weather, it stopped raining. And we wasted no time thinking about it. Our many volunteers immediately climbed up and wiped down the wall with dry rags, and we started spraying the first background colors.

I'd already contacted Steven Katona before the tour and asked him to be my consultant on the types of whales, dolphins, seals and other marine life that inhabit the Gulf of Maine and the coastline of the Northeast. I wanted to paint marine life that was found near each of the cities we'd be visiting. On the Portland wall, which was 1,000 feet long, I painted a humpback whale and her calf, finback whales, minke whales, white-sided dolphins, Atlantic bottlenose

Grand Marshall, Old Port Parade

Portsmouth press

Finishing Portsmouth, NH mural

With Steven Katona, Portland

Boston press conference

Diving Boston Harbor

Boston wall

Trucking through Time Square

With Roy Chavez before Today Show live from N.Y.

dolphins, sea lions and a loggerhead turtle.

When we were half-way done, the crowds were getting larger, and the city felt it was important we get some security — if only to keep the people away from me so I could work. We had created quite a frenzy. It was all very friendly, but it was becoming increasingly hard to paint because the crowd wanted autographs and to talk. I've always enjoyed that part of it, but the reality was that we had a huge wall to complete. So they hired a personal security guard to kind of keep the crowds back. I knew at that moment that this tour was going to be quite an experience.

To make things even more interesting, we had a cast of the most unusual bunch of characters who ever ventured into the unknown. When I selected these people to go on tour, it was like a whaling captain in the old days trying to entice men to join his crew. He would say, "Come and visit exotic ports, three square meals, women, wine. . . " It was recruiting, heavy recruiting. I fancied myself as much more than an Army or Marine recruiter. I was of the days of the whaling captain, enticing my crew to travel along on this voyage of exotic adven-

Wyland with school group, Portsmouth, NH

ture and pleasure and big bucks. Of course, none of it was true. The reality was 14-hour days, seven days a week for four solid months. I always say there's no rest when you are on planetary duty. And that, simply, was what it was — hard work and no rest. It made me think I might have been an old whaling captain reincarnated.

Regardless of whether or not I'd been a whaler in a previous life, my first mate on this voyage was Roy Chavez. We called him the "mayor" because he ran the painting activity around each of the walls. Roy has been painting with me since I painted the Redondo Beach wall in 1991. Ever since we painted that wall for Southern California Edison, where Roy works, he's been hooked. He has declared that he will continue to paint with me wherever and whenever I ask him. Without Roy assisting me in painting the backgrounds and preparing the walls and running my paint kitchen, it would have been impossible to have done anything on this scale.

I never had any doubts that this was going to be a long, grueling project. But even I underestimated how difficult it would be. By the time we hit Portsmouth, I had to give another Vince Lombardi speech. Mondays and Tuesdays became known as "Muesday," two marathon days that tested the wills and temperaments of the whole crew. They were exhausted because they had to tear everything down in one city, load up the truck and then unpack and set everything up for the next wall. Most of them had figured out that the exotic ports and women and food and all the things they'd been promised was a bunch of bull.

Actually, most of the crew were having a pretty

New London wall dedication

To share with you how crazy it is to be Wyland's spearhead, I am now sitting in my kitchen at midnight, sneaking some time away from planning the 1994 West Coast Tour and taking a moment to reminisce about the 1993 East Coast Tour. "17 murals, in 17 cities in 17 weeks" - Oh my! It was the miracle tour. They said it couldn't be done but we did it! I'll never forget the beginning planning; Wyland, Angela, Jim and I were sitting around Wyland's coffee table staring at my six inch Day Timer map. We brainstormed ideas with Wyland drinking more and more iced tea - consuming more and more caffeine. Anyone who has been around Wyland knows that he doesn't need any extra energy. He was now talking 100 mph and we outlined the entire tour all in one day. It was January 6, 1993 and Wyland's last words of the day were, "I'm ready. I could start tomorrow; but no, really, let's start June 1st". I had less than five months to find spearheads for each city, acquire national sponsors and finalize all seventeen wall sites. I was given an incredible challenge by Wyland and I knew in my heart that if I could share the energy of this incredible event with the people on the East Coast, the tour would materialize.

I became known as the "phone person," telling everyone about the tour including potential crew, Wyland collectors, animal groups, airlines, truck lines, paint companies, mayors, governors, etc... One by one, they started joining, not even knowing what was ahead of them. They all became a part of Team Wyland.

The East Coast Tour was an unbelievable, emotional and exciting tour that touched the hearts of millions of people. It will continue to touch them for the lifetime of Wyland's incredible gift - the murals.

Wyland is a guy with incredible vision and energy. Once he has an idea and he can see it, he makes it happen. I saw his vision of the East Coast Tour and it was an honor helping make it happen. I want to say "thank you" to our corporate staff, the crew, our sponsors, the volunteers and Wyland for making the tour a reality.
WE DID IT!

Sondra Augenstein

It all started with the Redondo Beach Whaling Wall. I was one of the painters that volunteered to assist Wyland in painting the mural. Before I had met him, I expected to be meeting a crusty old hard headed, beret wearing, paint slopping artist. Well, I was wrong. No crust, no beret and definitely no slopping paint. This guy knew how to control all the tools needed for the creation of a massive, emotionally charged mural.

Everybody involved was influenced by his genuine concern for our oceans and their inhabitants.

Wyland definitely wasn't what we expected. Instead we had a young bouncy, energetic, enthusiastic and down-to-earth kind of guy. This guy is never too busy to take time off from his work to speak to children about their local marine environment and the reason for his murals, plus there is always a question and answer time that seems to bring the artist and the children closer.

Because of Wyland, my way of thinking about our environment has taken a 180 degree turn. I figured whales would always be around and if they had a problem let some one else worry about it. I just didn't care. But now I know the importance of respecting and protecting the inhabitants of our oceans.

Wyland's Whaling Walls have the unique ability to bring people together. There are positive feelings of unity which seem to transcend a wide variety of ages and backgrounds. As each creation evolves it seems that the expectations and the moods of the onlookers become elevated much like a child's expectations when opening a beautifully wrapped gift at Christmas. The elation appears to build as the Wall's beauty unfolds and the marine subjects begin to take form. The marvel of Wyland's artistic talent and inviting presentation further enhances the experience. The expressive quality and artistic playfulness of the marine subjects project their peaceful aura upon the observers. The concrete wall comes to life as an ocean habitat. The enthusiasm rises as passive observations transform to heightened interest enhancing support and awareness of the endangered quality of the artist's subjects. The curious nature of the viewers often results in an expressed desire to become patrons of the cause. The atmosphere of the entire experience lends itself to strangers becoming friends and individuals becoming involved. Without exception, the marvel of Wyland's work is met with satisfaction and appreciation of the final outcome. The continued presence of the Whaling Walls serves to further fuel these feelings of positive regard and reflection. The song of the whale sings as long as the walls stand and the cry becomes heard by many who may never have heard it before.

---

good time. But I thought it was important that I tell them how I felt, that we weren't going to have time to visit the cities as tourists. The reality was that we were the attraction. We were the things the cities wanted to see. We were the event, and we should enjoy the journey and enjoy the moment.

The entire tour turned out to be a people tour as well as an art tour. We made great and lasting friends at every stop, getting to know the spirit of each of these places and communities. We were treated in each city as adopted sons, and most times we were given the key to the city. It truly was a team effort, and everybody felt good about it.

At the dedication ceremony for the Portsmouth wall, I received an urgent call from the Boston Police Department. They were concerned the media attention the Whaling Wall was generating might cause a major traffic problem on the 93 freeway, where they estimated a quarter of a million cars would drive past the wall each day. This was the most attractive thing to me: that millions of people a year would see these whales. The idea that the police were ready to cancel the project was very unnerving, and I was hurried to a backroom phone to talk to the frantic police officer in charge. I tried to low-key the event, but they knew better. They knew this was going to be major; it was already receiving heavy exposure from all of the Boston television and print media. I assured the officer that if traffic did get backed up, I would immediately disembark from the scaffolding and wait until it cleared. She finally relented and agreed to let the project begin.

The morning I was to start the Boston wall, I was invited for a dive by *Divers Down*, a national television show that features a celebrity diver once a year. They wanted me to dive, of all places, in Boston Harbor. They felt that if I could go out there and take a look at the harbor, that maybe I could incorporate some of that marine life into the mural. I felt it was a good opportunity to get wet so I agreed. I didn't realize that Boston Harbor was one of the most polluted bodies of water in the United States, and in the world for that matter. However, in the last five to ten years, there have been a lot of

Wildwood dedication ceremony

groups working to clean it up.

When we finished the dive, the police boat rushed me back to the dock so I could get to the press conference to announce the Boston Whaling Wall with John Walsh of the World Society for the Protection of Animals. After the press conference, Roy and I got on the scaffolding and immediately started painting masses of color. To my surprise, the first day we covered most of the wall with the background colors, the detail of the ocean's surface and the first life-size, breaching humpback. By the time the sun was setting, the mural looked like it was almost done. People were indeed backing up on the freeway, taking pictures, beeping their horns. I'd never seen so many cars nor felt so many eyes looking at me as I painted. But I seem to enjoy this kind of activity. The crazier it gets the better I paint. I could sense that this was going to be one of my best murals ever.

The next day, I painted another whale below the surface, a female humpback. I also painted something I'd been thinking about for years — a mother humpback pushing her calf to the surface for its first breath. Some of the volunteers, particularly in Doctor Roger Payne's crew, brought over some pictures of a humpback whale that had been seen off of the Massachusetts coastline, a place called Stellwagon Bank. It was a whale everybody knew as "Salt" because she had a white, salty patch on her dorsal fin. Humpback whales are unique in that they have tail markings that identify them as individuals. I had a chance to paint Salt's tail markings and her salty white patch on the dorsal fin and portray her individual features. Also, the fact that she was calving there nearly

Painting breaching whale, Wilmington, DE

It is a beautiful Hawaiian day, June 1, 1994. I have officially handed over the makings of Wyland's spectacular book, Celebrating 50 Wyland Whaling Walls to our Publishing Art director, Jennifer Mueller. This book brings to life the East Coast Tour as we lived it and with the completion of the book the journey has come full-circle. I can remember the first 'official' meeting in this very room when we saw "that gleam" in Wyland's eye, shining like a blue beacon. At that instant, I knew we were all about to take the ride of our lives! A tour of pure vision that became a big blue reality. This was, in the truest sense, a people tour. We literally met hundreds of thousands of people, from politicians and children to celebrities and Harley-Davidson clubs.

One of my favorite stories was when an energetic lady walked into Wyland's fine art exhibit in Myrtle beach, SC. She says to me, "One man does all this breathtaking art work and paints these life-size murals too?" "Yes", I replied and went on to tell her about his 17 murals, 17 cities, 17 week tour. "Unbelievable!" she exclaimed, "He sings too!"

Everyone becomes a part of Team Wyland. When my incredibly supportive family from Purcell, Oklahoma drove to join the team in Philadelphia, Pennsylvania they became instant moral boosters and pop-up volunteers. They enjoyed it so much they continued on to Wildwood, New Jersey for more tour fun. Thanks' guys!

Special thanks to Wyland, a Genius artiste, publisher, friend, and excellent dive buddy. Thank you for the "fabulous adventure" we live every single day!

Angela Eaton

My family in Wildwood, NJ

As the drivers for National Van Lines we had one of the best experiences in our life. We got the opportunity to pull Wyland's East Coast Tour. It was a privilege and an honor to work with him as well as get to know him.

We learned a lot about marine life as well as the environment. We take so much for granted. We believe that we are all put on this earth for a reason and everything is a vital part of this earth.

Watching Wyland work for 17 weeks was really amazing. Each week he made it look easier and easier. You would have to see for yourself to understand. Everything looks so real he captures the beauty and grace in everything that he paints and sculptures. He really has a God given talent.

Carlton and Trish Clark

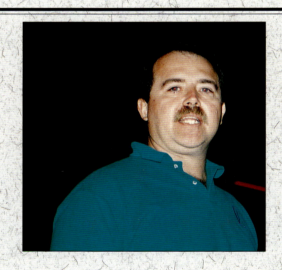

Wyland,
Moving to Hawaii to work for your brother Bill set me on a journey that I will never forget and always cherish. Hurricane Iniki took everything I owned, but the charity of your brother Bill made me feel like part of the family. Bill paid for housing, food and clothing, while my family and I got back onto our feet again........Thanks Bill.

Then you invited me to go on the East Coast Tour. Wyland, your perseverance and hard work, along with, of course, your talent, made everything a real joy. Even working with Sondra, who after working 12 hours in the heat would still complain if we sat down during loading !! Oh, and rooming with Michael Murray, the white version of Don King!!! All kidding aside though, thanks for the greatest experience of my life!!

Fred (the bone) Mongeon

every year was very special in the painting of her portrait. The mural became not only a life-size portrait of humpback whales, but a picture of an actual whale that had been studied and photographed for over 20 years.

Boston had the foresight to light the mural, which would be seen 24 hours a day by over 250,000 cars a day. It was going to be one of the most visible murals in the world. We had a special lighting ceremony the night before the dedication. When they flicked the switch for the lights, the mural became three-dimensional. It was like a night dive, hard to describe. We drove on the freeway back and forth several times, it was stunning.

In Providence, Rhode Island, the wall went without a hitch. But New York City was a completely different story. We had originally found the perfect wall at the Jacob Javitts Convention Center, which was actually the vent tower for the New York Port Authority Lincoln Tunnel Ventilation Building. After tons of negotiations, we were all ready to sign the paperwork, and Sondra flew to New York with the contract. As luck would have it, the timing couldn't have been worse. The day before, the World Trade Center was bombed by terrorists, and the Port Authority of New York and New Jersey's offices were housed there. Their executives were concerned that if I painted this mural, it would become a target due to all of the media coverage on the Whaling Wall. Already scheduled were Bryant Gumbel of NBC's *Today Show*, along with CBS and *Good Morning America*. All three major networks were going to cover us live from New York, which made the Port Authority very nervous.

I found out later I would've been blown right out of that tower wall on the fourth of July as the terrorist had planned. But I was determined more than ever to do a wall in New York, and we were able to find another site 48 hours before I was to start painting. We drove to New York City late at night and pulled up to the Port Authority of New York and New Jersey Bus Terminal on 41st Street, probably one of the ugliest and most crime-ridden, drug-trafficking, murderous, crack-head, inner-city locations in New York. I literally

With Very Special Arts' kids, National Zoo - Washington, D.C.

had to step over people living in boxes to get to the site. As I looked at the wall, I decided that if any environment in the world needed changing, this was it. The wall was part of a dark, black tunnel between the two bus terminals. I must admit I was nervous painting this mural without a bulletproof vest. The scene going on behind me included fist fights between husbands, wives and pimps. People were doing crack in broad daylight.

We worked hard every single day, and it was progressing nicely with some humpback whales. The following morning I was to go on the *Today Show* live at 6 a.m. Jim Fowler, of Mutual of Omaha's *Wild Kingdom* fame, and a friend of mine from years past, was going to come down and interview me. So it was challenging to get the wall to look like something in one day. I raced as fast as I could to cover all the background colors and try to at least get one whale up there. I finished half of the whale the first day. It was probably 2 a.m. and, in that neighborhood, this was quite an experience. The people in the area at that time of morning were not the kind you'd want to hang around with. I had most of my crew around me, watching my back.

We finally got back to the Paramount Hotel, managed a couple of hours sleep and returned at 5 a.m., not only for the *Today Show*, but for *CBS Live*. When I got down there, the network news crews had already been there, and it looked like a major motion picture set with lights, cameras, makeup crews and my buddy, Jim Fowler. His was the only familiar face in a sea of TV people. He was very warm and pleasant, and his wife, Betsy, an artist and good friend of mine, was also there.

Jim and I were set to air live when Bryant Gumbel said: "Hey, Wyland, why did you pick this wall in New York? Are there any whales in New York?" I said there were and, fortunately, Jim helped me out: "Yes, Bryant, we once had the humpback whales Wyland has depicted right here in the Hudson River." Then Bryant asked me if we were raising money near the wall and, if so, what were we doing with it. "Well, Bryant, we're not trying to raise money. . .

Official dedication, Baltimore wall

Being involved with the East Coast Tour was educational and fun. Going into all the different cities, seeing many scenic areas and meeting interesting people was a great experience. With Wyland's encouragement and desire for his team to be certified in deep sea diving it became possible for us to explore a whole new world under the sea.
Wyland has always cared about the environment and enjoys teaching what he's learned to all people with much focus on kids and other interested artists.
Overall we liked traveling, working with family, making new friends and being a part of Team Wyland.

Thomas and Valerie Wyland

Having been employed by Wyland Galleries for 3 years now and having worked with Wyland during the creation of 18 walls, I'd have to say I have a unique perspective of Wyland the artist and Wyland the man.
First and foremost is his unbelievable energy. He always works on solutions and not problems. During the four month East Coast Tour his energy was incredible - everyone else on tour was worn out and ready for a vacation and he was still going. Not only did he paint the murals, but Wyland met the press cheerfully. He supervised all photography and video, interacted with all the tour members, oversaw finances and made all final decisions - always with a smile and a sincerity that contributes to the special Wyland mystique - and it's just that - a powerful, charismatic, positive presence that endears him to children and adults of all varieties. Wyland treats everyone the same - and he really listens to people - and that cannot be said of too many people on this planet.
My favorite part of every mural is watching Wyland come off the scaffolding with a big smile on his face waving to the school children. He spends more time with children than with anyone. It's amazing to watch the dynamics at work - and the kids walk away feeling they can make a difference.

Mike Murray

When I was first asked to be on the East Coast Tour I was a little skeptical. Although it seemed like a great opportunity, seventeen weeks would be a long time to stay away from surfing. Even though Wyland promised me fortune, fame, women and great east coast surfing, I had my doubts.

The work on the tour was long and grueling — from cleaning a wall in a not so great location of New York until 2:00 am to setting up outdoor exhibits in 100 degree weather.

Even though the work was tough, it was well worth it. Getting a chance to help Wyland raise environmental awareness across the eastern seaboard was incredible. The best was meeting all sorts of different people who cared for our environment as much as we did, and then watching them be touched by Wyland and his walls. I really feel through helping Wyland that I have done a part in trying to save the same ocean I surf in.

The highlight of the tour was when I met my now fiancee, Darcelle, in Maine and she traveled with me for the rest of the tour. I even got to surf - thanks to Hurricane Emily. So you could say the East Coast Tour was definitely worth it.

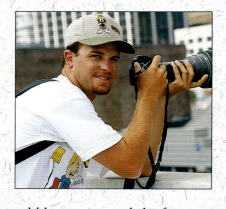

No one could have prepared the fourteen of us for what we experienced on the East Coast. Most days were long and hard ones; composed of many make-or-break situations that demanded improvisation and a lot of creativity. To this day many of us still have a hard time believing that we did it. But we did. While looking at some of the pictures I have taken of the crew, I noticed that each one of us looks nothing alike. We were all very different and that made each day more interesting and made the tour more of a learning experience than a working one.

I think what amazed me the most about our trip from Maine to Key West was that each time we pulled into a new town, there were dozens of friendly and eager faces ready to help turn a normal building side into artwork that might help save their own coastline.

Erik Hansen

we're trying to raise consciousness," I said.

After 15 minutes on NBC, I ran over and did another 15 with CBS. As soon as they left, we got back to work and completed the mural in only five days. I dedicated the wall to Jim Fowler, whom I enjoyed for many years on *Wild Kingdom* when I was growing up. He came back and signed it with me during a special ceremony on July 5th.

We were really looking forward to the next wall in the old whaling village of New London, Connecticut. What we weren't looking forward to, however, was the intense heat wave that had just moved in. It had already killed over 100 people, and the heat generated off the wall was right in my face. Angela suffered a heat stroke, and Roy caught her just before she hit the pavement. A couple of hours later, I suffered heat stroke, too, for the first time in my life. My legs wobbled and caved in, and I had to be taken where there was some air conditioning and wet rags to recover.

After New London, we painted a very high wall in Philadelphia that had exceptional visibility from all parts of downtown, including the Amtrak Station. We then did a mural in Wildwood, New Jersey, which, ecstatic over being chosen over Atlantic City for a Whaling Wall, was the most enthusiastic of all the cities on the tour. Hundreds of thousands of people came down to see the wall, including thousands of kids I could talk to and teach about whales. The Harley-Davidson Riders of New Jersey also came down and gave me a jacket and loaned me a Harley to ride.

Our next stop was Wilmington, Delaware, where I painted a diptych showing only above water scenes. Then we moved on to Washington, D.C., where I painted a mural at the Smithsonian Institute's National Zoo. Even though this was the smallest wall on the tour, we called it the "Mighty Wall" because it was right at the entrance to the zoo. Five million people would walk right by it every year. The dedication was attended by world-renowned whale researcher Dr. Roger Payne and many in Washington's political circles. A Congressional Record from Hawaii Senator Dan Inouye read: "Wyland is considered by many to be the finest environmental artist in the world."

I had wanted to do a mural on the National Aquarium in Baltimore for a long time. But, when we got there, we came across the aquarium director, Nick Brown, who in my opinion, had no vision whatsoever. A marine mural on the aquarium was not his idea, so it didn't have his blessing or approval. What was ironic was that I had just finished a wall at the National Zoo, and here was the National Aquarium — the most

Painting seven stories above, Norfolk, VA

appropriate place to have a Whaling Wall — and its director was trying to stop the mural. He had influenced a lot of city officials, including the architect, and together they opposed the project. We were running out of time so we started with the wall across the street from Camden Yards. This site was very attractive and would actually see more traffic on the main road than the National Aquarium. But I still think the aquarium was the most appropriate, and I intend to paint a mural there one day. All I need is their blessing.

The Baltimore mural was the first time I'd painted an extinct species of whales, the Atlantic gray whales, which were wiped out in the early 17th century by American Yankee whalers. I wanted to bring attention to this fact with an extinction mural. It raised a lot of questions. Anytime you can tell a story and get your message across, then you're doing what you're supposed to do with your art. In Norfolk, Virginia, I was battling the flu and seriously wondering if I could finish their wall in just six days. The wall was over 260 feet long and eight stories high. The tour was starting to take its toll. Somehow, though, Roy, the crew and I worked all day, every day, and the mural turned out to be one of my best. Tens of thousands of people came down to see the mural in progress, and it was fun to watch the police from our sixth-story perch putting up yellow tape to control the crowd. Then they took that down and put up some wooden barriers and, eventually, closed down the whole street. Afterward, we dedicated the wall to Jacques Cousteau and visited The Cousteau Society in nearby Chesapeake, Virginia.

We quickly finished a small wall in Wilmington, North Carolina. We had picked a larger wall earlier, but the mayor caved in to a small group, and we ended up painting a postage stamp mural instead of a real Whaling Wall. The mural turned out really nice, though, and thousands of people made the pilgrimage to Wilmington to watch me paint it.

Then we drove to Myrtle Beach, our 14th mural in 14 weeks. We were

With Mandy Rodriquez and Flow

Crew set-up

Thousands attend official dedication, Norfolk, VA

Painting humpback fluke markings, NJ

Wyland with Boston spearhead, John Walsh and Flipper, WSPA

Visiting friendly dolphins, Dolphin Research Center, FL

Talking with group in Sarasota, FL

exhausted, but we could see the light at the end of the tunnel. The people of Myrtle Beach were very warm, just like the city. School was coming into session, and they were busing kids in for this public art event. Whenever I saw a group down there, I would go down and spend time with them. At one point, about 600 kids came to meet me. What was great was that they knew more about marine art and saving the ocean than I ever did at their age. Some of them are even better artists than I was. And that's always encouraging to me. They get so excited and are so honest about everything; I wish more adults would be like these kids. We figured that by the end of the tour, I'd talked to over 70,000 kids! To me, that was what this tour was all about.

I painted right whales at Myrtle Beach, the first time I'd done this in the States. It was appropriate because they had right whales off the South Carolina coast. The last right whales I'd painted were in Taiji, Japan. The Myrtle Beach mural really was quite easy and seemed to paint itself. With all the support of the community and volunteers, it was a good time.

Everyone was excited when we reached Atlanta. At the opening ceremony, Atlanta Mayor Maynard Jackson spoke of the mural's importance to the city. This was our 50th Whaling Wall, the half-way mark in my goal of painting 100 around the world. It was a huge wall, 450 feet long and over seven stories high, one of the largest murals in the Eastern United States. It fronted the Coca-Cola museum and had tremendous visibility from all parts of the city. Hopefully, with the Olympics coming to Atlanta, it'll be one of the best landmarks in the city.

In Sarasota, the Mote Marine Laboratory had wanted me to do a Whaling Wall for several years. Mike Martin, who is a good friend and happens to be on the board of directors there, coordinated this project. I felt it was very important to do a mural for this new marine mammal facility they had built to help stranded marine mammals. When I was about to finish this mural, I invited Mike to come up on the scaffolding since he had spearheaded the project. We weren't up there 10 minutes, and all we had to do was paint a few fish and the mural would be finished. Mike suddenly turned to hand me a brush and accidentally kicked a can of black paint and it went all over the whole mural. His face turned white. He was frantic, but I was laughing. I just said it looked like seagrass to me. It covered the entire bottom half of the wall with black. I got down and tried to hose it off, but it was too late. So I incorpo-

East coast tour crew, Sarasota, FL

rated it into the seagrass and named him as an assistant painter.

We finally made it down to Key West, one of my favorite towns in Florida and in all of the United States. I love the Keys for diving and have spent a lot of my vacations down there looking at America's only living reef on the mainland. I'd already painted a wall in Marathon Keys a few years earlier, but Key West was where it was at. We were working with a very well known group called Reef Relief, which had done some great work to design buoys to protect the reef, replacing anchors that would damage it. They were also involved in a lot of clean water efforts and were to spearhead the Whaling Wall project. Unfortunately, the wall I wanted to paint on the Waterfront Playhouse was shot down by a small group of people. Reef Relief found another location, though, that was actually larger. They felt it would become a major landmark after the mural was completed. And sure enough, the Coach Train made it part of their daily tours.

My crew and I were relieved just to be in Key West, knowing this was the last mural on the tour and we would get a well deserved rest. I told everyone they could have a week off when we were done, on me, and they were sure ready for it after a long hot summer.

When I saw the wall at the Waterfront Market, I immediately envisioned Florida's living reef. I'd been thinking about it for years. The wall was not very large, but in a good location. The mural had a huge impact and became a local favorite as soon as we started painting.

Key West was fantastic. Captain Tony, the former mayor and co-owner of Captain Tony's, and a good friend of Jimmy Buffet's, came down and dedicated the wall with the current mayor. It was dedicated to the people of Key West and to Reef Relief and their efforts. Spirits were high. We were ready to enjoy Key West and then get back home. After four months of working sunup to sundown, living in hotel rooms and being in the public eye, I was ready to go down to the Caribbean and enjoy some quality time underwater.

Only a few weeks later, I was already thinking about a West Coast Tour. . . exotic ports, beautiful women, great food. I'll tell ya, if it weren't for the money, the women (whales) and the time off, I'd have nothing to do with this job. . . Just kidding!

Volunteers mixing tons of paint

With fans in Norfolk, VA

Atlanta Whaling Wall 50

Celebrating 50 walls, Atlanta's Hard Rock Cafe

With Captain Tony in Key West, FL

WHALING WALL 36
WHALES OFF THE GULF OF MAINE

The first stop on Wyland's formidable 17-mural, 17-city, 17-week East Coast Tour got off to a slippery start in Portland, Maine. On Tuesday, June 1, with everything in place and ready to go, the artist, his crew and the township of Portland had to wait out a cold, pelting rainstorm before the first dab of paint could be applied to the side of the Bath Iron Works, opposite the Maine State Pier.

"How about a rain dance?" Wyland said at last, standing beneath one of the press tents that had been erected for the event. Realizing he only had six days to complete the mural before flying to the next city on the tour, he ran out onto the pier and danced a jig in the midst of the downpour. Half an hour later, the rain slowed and soon stopped altogether. Team Wyland wasted no time. They climbed up, wiped the wall down and started spraying paint.

"Before we even flew to Portland, I had contacted my friend Steven Katona, a leading marine mammal scientist from the College of the Atlantic, to find out what types of whales, dolphins, seals and other marine life inhabited the Gulf of Maine and, for that matter, the entire coastline," the artist recalls.

Just in time for Sunday's Old Port Festival, in which he served as Grand Marshal, Wyland completed the mural. Measuring about 1,000 feet in length, the wall had become the ocean habitat for a mother humpback whale and her calf, finback whales, minke whales, white-sided dolphins, Atlantic bottlenose dolphins, sea lions and a loggerhead turtle.

Many of the Southern Maine residents who attended the festival that Sunday confessed that the foul weather would have kept them home had it not been for the Whaling Wall. As it turned out, tens of thousands braved the rain all week to visit the wall and see the Maine State Pier transformed into the state's newest landmark.

WHALING WALL 37
ISLE OF SHOALS HUMPBACKS

By the time Wyland reached Portsmouth, New Hampshire, the second city scheduled on the East Coast Tour, the artist and his crew knew they were in for a long, grueling 17 weeks. But the community's exuberance and genuine interest in the Whaling Wall project picked up their spirits, resulting in a beautiful mural for the people of this city.

"This mural was critical to the tour because it was the first test of how fast we could finish a wall in one city and move on to the next city and get started," Wyland recalls. "It was a real challenge, but we met it and were on our way. The reaction of the people of Portsmouth really helped to rejuvenate us."

Portsmouth Mayor Eileen Foley presented Wyland with the key to the city, and the Shoals Marine Laboratory at the University of New Hampshire started a fund-raising scholarship program in the artist's name. "I was especially proud of the fund-raiser," Wyland says. "The money will be used to start a lectureship about marine mammals in the Gulf of Maine."

The mural, painted on two walls of the Cabot House furniture store facing the Vaughn Mall parking lot, depicts three humpback whales that frequent the local waters, as well as a family of dolphins and a school of tuna.

"I must have talked to everyone in this town, especially the children," Wyland claims. "If I didn't, I'm hoping the Whaling Wall will."

Whaling Wall XXXVII — Portsmouth, New Hampshire — 220 feet long x 40 feet high — Dedicated June 14, 1993 by Mayor Eileen Foley

Finishing Portsmouth mural

photo by Jock Montgomery

Proclamation from the Mayor

Standing by lifesize finback whale

Signing Portland wall

▲ **Whaling Wall XXXVI** — Portland, Maine — 1,000 feet long x 25 feet high — Dedicated June 7, 1993 by Steven Katona

WHALING WALL 38
STELLWAGON BANK HUMPBACKS

Painting a Whaling Wall in Boston, Massachusetts, was especially appealing to Wyland because of the prominent city's long association with whaling. But the wall chosen for the mural, the side of the Summerfield Building just south of the South Station tunnel, offered an additional opportunity. Located on Travelers Street next to Highway 93, over a quarter of a million cars would pass by the mural each day.

"This wall is exceptional not only because of its size, 12 1/2 stories high and 120 feet wide," Wyland explains "but its location means that millions of people will be exposed to the beauty of living humpback whales. This is exactly what I'm trying to accomplish with the Whaling Walls: to raise the consciousness of as many people as I can about the need to preserve these majestic creatures."

Capturing the attention of millions of motorists, however, proved to be something that also was hard to ignore by the Boston Police Department. In fact, even before Team Wyland reached Boston, the department had called Wyland and voiced their concern that the media attention the tour was generating might create a major traffic jam on the Boston freeway.

"I was scared the police might shut the project down before it even got started," the artist recalls. "I was anxious to get to Boston, climb up on the scaffolding and paint the first whale as soon as possible so people would see what I was doing and support the mural."

And that's exactly what happened. Working closely with John Walsh and volunteers from the Society for the Protection of Animals, Wyland and his crew painted all of the background colors and a breaching humpback on the first day. The female humpback was a replica of an actual whale named Salt that had been studied and photographed off the Massachusetts coastline for over 20 years. Wyland then painted something into the mural he had wanted to paint for years — a mother humpback pushing her calf to the surface for a breath of air.

The mural was heavily publicized, and many cars did slow down to watch it being painted, but the momentum behind it was infectious, and even the police liked it. "When we finished, the City lit the mural at a special lighting ceremony, which gave it a three-dimensional quality," Wyland says. "At that point, everyone sensed that we had created something very special."

WHALING WALL 39
FINBACK WHALES

In some instances during the East Coast Tour, Wyland found it necessary to become personally involved in securing a site for one of his Whaling Walls. Normally, the wall and most, if not all, of the permits necessary for the project would be cleared in advance by city officials. In Providence, Rhode Island, however, the artist had to find a wall himself during the few short hours he was in town during his press tour to announce wall sites.

"The Providence city officials had yet to find a wall so I piled them into our van and drove them down the highway looking for a wall," Wyland recalls. "We'd barely started driving down the freeway when I spotted what looked to be a great location. The wall was quite long but not very high.

Wyland pulled the van into the parking lot of the building where the wall was, the Cassiere Machinery Company, and went in to talk to the owner. The "luck of the whale" was with the artist, as the owner, Joseph Cassiere, turned out to be an admirer of whales who actually had figures of the marine mammals on his desk. He agreed, the city agreed, and it was done. The mural, bearing finback whales, was completed in time for the Providence Waterfront Festival, helping to draw tens of thousands to the event.

Whaling Wall XXXIX — Providence, Rhode Island — 280 feet long x 24 feet high — Dedicated June 28, 1993 by Mayor Vincent Cianci

Painting Humpback, Boston, MA

▲ **Whaling Wall XXXVIII** — Boston, Massachusetts — 110 feet long x 125 feet high — Dedicated June 21, 1993 by John Walsh, President of WSPA

WHALING WALL 40
INNER CITY WHALES

Selecting and gaining approval to paint a Whaling Wall in New York City presented a new set of challenges that could only be found in The Big Apple. Wyland had initially selected the "perfect" wall at the Jacob Javitts Convention Center. But the site fell through when the World Trade Center was suddenly bombed by terrorists. The Port Authority of New York, whose vent tower was located at the convention center, then decided the Whaling Wall might become targeted by the terrorists.

However, they helped Wyland's team find another wall at the Port Authority Bus Terminal on the 41st Street underpass. "This area was one of the worst in the city," Wyland says. "Crime, drugs, winos, prostitution — it was horrible. I felt the real challenge was going to be how I could add something positive to such a dreary environment."

With his crew watching his back, the artist quickly painted humpback whales swimming along the low 450-foot-long tunnel between the two bus terminals. The mural was showcased by all three major networks, including *The Today Show* and *Good Morning America*. After five days of painting, it was dedicated by Jim Fowler, of Mutual of Omaha's *Wild Kingdom*.

"The attention this mural drew was tremendous," Wyland acknowledges. "A lot of people will see it every day. The only thing I would change about it, though, would be the lighting. I hope the Port Authority will one day replace the dim, yellow lights in that tunnel with lights that'll really enhance this beautiful mural in the inner city."

With Jim Fowler, N.Y. ▶

WHALING WALL 41
THE GREAT SPERM WHALES

After New York, Wyland and his crew were looking forward to moving on to the smaller town of New London, Connecticut. Not only was it a small community, it also had a long history of whaling, having been, at one point in the mid-1800's, one of the busiest whaling ports on the East Coast.

"I especially like to paint Whaling Walls in these cities because they have such a rich heritage in maritime history," Wyland explains. "With the exception of Japan, Norway and a few other countries, whaling has been replaced by whale watching, which many old whaling villages have found to be very healthy for tourism and economic development."

Despite a New England summer heat wave that caused Wyland to have to come down off the wall and receive treatment for heat stroke, the New London wall went, as the artist put it, "swimmingly." The mural, depicting a family of sperm whales, Connecticut's state mammal, helped to draw up to 250,000 people to New London's Sail Fest, the city's annual maritime festival, prompting the mayor to name July 6-12 "Wyland Week." The landmark mural was dedicated by Governor Lowell Weiker, who presented the artist with a special proclamation.

Whaling Wall XL — New York, New York — 460 feet long x 22 feet high — Dedicated July 5, 1993 by Jim Fowler, Mutual Omaha's "Wild Kingdom"

Enjoying New York

Painting sperm whales

Measuring life-size sperm whales

Connecticut Governor Weiker dedicating New London mural

▲ **Whaling Wall XLI** — New London, Connecticut — 170 feet long x 35 feet high — Dedicated July 12, 1993 by Governor Lowell Weiker

WHALING WALL 42
EAST COAST HUMPBACKS

Center City's Marketplace Design Center in Philadelphia was the perfect location for the next Whaling Wall on the tour. Standing 130 feet high and 125 feet long, it enjoys exceptional visibility from all parts of downtown Philadelphia.

"I wanted to paint a large wall in Philadelphia because it's probably fair to say that most of the citizens of this fine city had never laid eyes on a real whale, much less several whales that were life-size," Wyland says. "This mural now gives them that opportunity and, hopefully, brings to their attention the majesty of these creatures and the need to do everything we can to préserve them."

"Philadelphia also has a rich history in public art," he adds. "I felt that a Whaling Wall would be a beautiful addition to the city and help raise awareness about the plight of whales at the same time."

Although the wall was interrupted by several windows, the canvas was more than large enough for Wyland to paint three life-size humpback whales — a mother, her calf and another adult — along with two Atlantic bottlenose dolphins and a school of tuna.

WHALING WALL 43
HUMPBACKS OFF THE JERSEY COAST

The citizenry of Wildwood, New Jersey, went wild when Wyland came to town to paint this mural. Accustomed to seeing nearby Atlantic City and its famous boardwalk receive publicity for decades, Wildwood was ecstatic over being chosen for a Whaling Wall.

Wyland had selected Wildwood, in fact, because the community was so enthusiastic over the project and the summer tourism trade promised increased visibility. As he painted, literally hundreds of thousands of people came to see the wall and, as usual, Wyland took time out to talk to the children and teach them about whales.

"I'll usually stop what I'm doing to talk to kids," the artist says. "They have a natural curiosity about the ocean and its creatures, and they'll be the ones who will inherit the responsibility to preserve them."

During the week, over 150 handicapped and disadvantaged children were bused from New York to watch Wyland paint the mural, which depicts humpback whales, dolphins, tuna and sea turtles — all seen off the New Jersey Coast.

▲ **Whaling Wall XLIII** — Wildwood, New Jersey — 220 feet long x 30 feet high — Dedicated July 26, 1993 by Mayor Edmund Grant

Painting Wildwood wall

Talking to Philadelphia art students

Painting Philadelphia wall

▲ **Whaling Wall XLII** — Philadelphia, Pennsylvania — 175 feet long x 130 feet high — Dedicated July 19, 1993 by Mayor Edward Rendall

WHALING WALL 44
DELAWARE MARINE MAMMALS

The front of Architects Studio on Market Street in Wilmington, Delaware, presented a special challenge for Wyland because the two walls were dissected by a wide external stairwell.

"This mural is essentially a diptych with two fairly vertical surfaces," he explains. "To achieve more continuity on either side of the stairwell, I decided the mural would work better if both sides were above-the-surface paintings. So I painted a humpback in full breach out of the water on the left side, and a school of bottlenose dolphins skipping on the ocean's surface on the right side."

Situated near Wilmington's Christina waterfront, which, in the `1860s to `1880s, was the launch for whaling ships going up the river and through a bay to reach the Atlantic, the mural is seen daily by people passing by on Amtrak. According to members of the Wilmington Arts Commission, the Whaling Wall will help revive the troubled waterfront district by giving it a fresh new look and message of hope.

"Painting a Whaling Wall in a non-coastal city always gives me an opportunity to reach people who would not normally be thinking about whales," Wyland says. "My intention is to expose as many people as I can to these animals so they'll join, in whatever way they can, the movement to save our oceans and marine life."

WHALING WALL 45
DOLPHINS, SMALL-TOOTH WHALES

While the mural at the National Zoo in Washington, D.C., is the smallest Whaling Wall Wyland has painted, the artist considers it one of his most important. Painted on a wall right at the front entrance to the zoo, it is estimated that five million people will walk by it every year.

Because of its size, only 30 feet long and 15 feet high, Wyland decided to paint the smallest of whales — dolphins, which are actually small-tooth whales. "When I told him I was going to paint dolphins at the zoo, Dr. Roger Payne, the world's leading whale researcher, recommended I paint the harbor porpoise, the smallest of the dolphins," Wyland says. "I thought it was a great idea and painted one in his honor. He flew over from London to dedicate the mural, which was a great honor for me."

Several political dignitaries attended the dedication ceremony as well, and the triangle-shaped mural drew accolades from the World Wildlife Fund and the National Wildlife Federation, among others. While in Washington, the artist also presented the Very Special Arts gallery with an original painting to be made into a print to help raise funds for artists with disabilities.

▲ Whaling Wall XLVIV — Wilmington, Delaware — 90 feet long x 60 feet high — Dedicated August 2, 1993 by Mayor Jim Sills & Senator Bill Roth

Official dedication

Dr. Roger Payne at dedication ceremony

Small but mighty wall

Painting "First Breath" oil at National Zoo

Dedication ceremony

▲ **Whaling Wall XLV** — Washington, D.C. — 30 feet long x 15 feet high — Dedicated August 9, 1993 by Dr. Roger Payne

WHALING WALL 46
EXTINCT ATLANTIC GRAY WHALES

Wyland originally planned to paint a mural on the National Aquarium in Baltimore, Maryland, something he had wanted to do for a long time. But the Aquarium declined, saying the project first had to be approved by Baltimore's Architectural Review Board, which would take more time than the artist could afford to spend in Baltimore.

Even though he had already picked out a wall at the Aquarium, Wyland had to find another site — the Lee Electric Building at Hamburg and Russell Streets. The long wall is visible to anyone driving in or out of the city along Russell Street.

"I decided to paint the Atlantic gray whale, which had been hunted to extinction in the early 1700's," the artist says. "This was the first time I'd painted an extinct species, but I wanted to pay homage to the whales and raise awareness about the fact that an entire population or species can be wiped out by man."

As for the National Aquarium? "It's not over," Wyland warns. "What better place could there be for a Whaling Wall than the National Aquarium? Everything I would paint on the wall would be in complete harmony with the Aquarium. It's not necessary to have whales and dolphins in captivity today, but appreciating them through life-size art makes perfect sense. In fact, I've already painted this mural in my mind."

WHALING WALL 47
HUMPBACKS OFF THE VIRGINIA COAST

Wyland was battling the flu when he pulled into Norfolk, Virginia. When he gazed up at the wall selected for the mural he was unsure about whether he would have the stamina to complete the project in just six days. It was one of the largest walls on the tour, 260 feet long and 60 feet high.

However, when Norfolk Mayor Mason Andrews declared the first day "Wyland Day" at the opening press conference, the fatigued artist grabbed a second wind and worked from dusk to dawn until the mural was finished.

"Tens of thousands of people came down to watch, and the police had to put up barriers to control the crowds," Wyland recalls. "I was sore all over from the flu, but there was something about thousands of people watching every move I made while I worked. It was very motivational — to the point where the aches and pains no longer mattered."

The entire city embraced the Whaling Wall and, with the help of many dedicated local volunteers, it was finished at sunset on the sixth and final day.

The mural depicts humpbacks, dolphins and tuna and is visible both from the Elizabeth River and Waterside Drive. Wyland dedicated the Whaling Wall to Jacques Cousteau, who had inspired him as a youth to focus on whales and marine life as his art subjects. While in Norfolk, Wyland visited the Cousteau Society in Chesapeake, Virginia, where he was greeted by a very friendly staff. He left one of his bronze sculptures as a gift to Mr. Cousteau, who wrote him a personal "thank you" letter.

Whaling Wall XLVI — Baltimore, Maryland — 260 feet long x 20 feet high — Dedicated August 16, 1993 by Mayor Kurt L. Schmoke

Ready to paint Baltimore wall

▲ **Whaling Wall XLVII** — Norfolk, Virginia — 280 feet long x 80 feet high — Dedicated August 23, 1993 by Mayor Mason Andrews

Norfolk crew

Dedication day crowds

Newest Norfolk landmark

WHALING WALL 48
COASTAL DOLPHINS

Although a large wall had been initially selected for a Whaling Wall in Wilmington, North Carolina, the site fell through in the approval process and was replaced by a much smaller wall.

"I remember telling the press that this was a 'postage stamp' compared to my other murals," Wyland says. "But the painting turned out very nice, and thousands of people came to see it. I was very pleased with the way everything turned out. I also enjoyed talking with the many kids who were brought to the mural site by their teachers."

The mural, which required only 50 gallons of paint, portrays local Atlantic bottlenose dolphins playing off the North Carolina coastline. After talking with local sea turtle experts, Wyland also added a threatened loggerhead turtle swimming beneath the cavorting dolphins.

"I do my best work when I start a mural with no preconceived idea," Wyland says. "This gives me the flexibility to learn more about the local environment and just let the marine life swim into the oceans I paint on the walls."

Whaling Wall XLVIII — Wilmington, North Carolina — 40 feet long x 30 feet high — Dedicated August 30, 1993 by Mayor Don Betz

Signing mural

WHALING WALL 49
RIGHT WHALES OFF THE SOUTH CAROLINA COAST

This mural in Myrtle Beach, South Carolina, was Team Wyland's 14th mural in 14 weeks, and the artist and his crew had the tour's routine down to where everything went like clockwork.

"This mural almost painted itself," Wyland says. "What was nice about the work going so smoothly was that I had a chance to talk to thousands of children. At one point, I think 600 kids came to watch me paint. School had just started, and they were busing children in from everywhere!"

One seventh-grade schoolteacher brought her class to the wall to discuss whales with Wyland. "They beat me to the punches," he laughs. "They knew a lot more about marine life than I ever did at their age, and that reinforces my belief that we still have a chance to save the whales and our oceans."

Wyland painted right whales on the mural because, even though they're the most endangered of the whale species, they can occasionally be seen off the South Carolina coast. Three right whales — a mother, her calf and another adult — now swim across the 250-foot-long wall along with four bottlenose dolphins.

With 600 Myrtle Beach kids

Myrtle Beach wall dedication

▲ **Whaling Wall XLIX** — Myrtle Beach, South Carolina — 250 feet long x 50 high — Dedicated September 13, 1993 by Mayor Bob Grisom

WHALING WALL 50
ATLANTA'S RIGHT WHALES

Atlanta's was the milestone everyone traveling on the East Coast Tour was waiting for. Not only would it be one of the largest murals in the country, it would be Wyland's 50th Whaling Wall, the half-way point in his extraordinary goal of painting 100 Whaling Walls by the year 2011.

"Atlanta is where the 1996 Olympics will be held, and this mural, with its exceptional size and location, should be very visible to millions of people," Wyland says of the 450-foot, seven-story Whaling Wall.

Painted on the side of Underground Atlanta and fronting the Coca-Cola museum, the gigantic mural portrays four right whales swimming in a vast blue ocean. One of the whales is suspended upright spyhopping, which is what whales do when they want to take a look around above the surface.

Atlanta's Hard Rock Cafe gave Team Wyland a public reception and collected his painter's pants, T-shirt, hat and shoes to be framed for their collection.

"It was really gratifying to reach 50 Whaling Walls," the artist admits. "This 17-mural tour helped push me in my endeavor to paint 100 Whaling Walls, and it's always a boost when you get over the hump. Only 50 more to go."

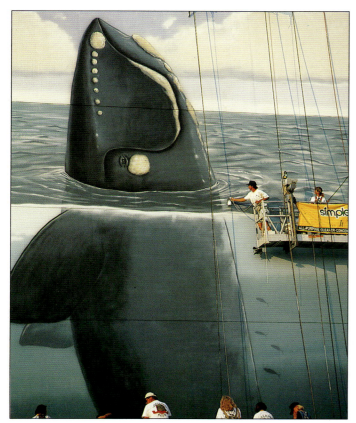
Painting right whale spyhopping

▲ **Whaling Wall L** — Atlanta, Georgia — 450 feet long x 50 high — Dedicated September 13, 1993 by Mayor Maynard Jackson

WHALING WALL 51
FLORIDA'S BOTTLENOSE DOLPHINS

The Mote Marine Laboratory in Sarasota, Florida, had been asking Wyland to paint a mural there for several years, and the East Coast Tour presented the perfect opportunity for the artist to accommodate their request.

"I was especially interested in doing a mural for the laboratory because I wanted to draw attention to the new facility they'd built to help stranded marine mammals," Wyland says, referring to the new Ann and Alfred Goldstein Marine Mammal Research and Rehabilitation Center on Center Island. "I felt that the spirit of this wall was special because the facility is intended to help the animals."

The wall was not all that large so Wyland chose to paint bottlenose dolphins, a native species that one day will probably be supported at the marine mammal facility. Randy Wells, one of the top dolphin researchers in the country, invited Wyland to observe the local dolphins in the wild. Later, he joined the artist on his scaffolding to paint individual dolphins he had studied over the years.

In appreciation for his efforts, the City of Sarasota declared September 15-19 "Wyland Week" and made him an honorary citizen. The artist responded by declaring that he will set up a foundation for a scholarship to Ringling Art School, one of the top-rated art schools in the country.

WHALING WALL 52
FLORIDA'S LIVING REEF

The Key West Whaling Wall was the last mural on the East Coast Tour, and the members of Team Wyland were exuberant that they were about to reach the finish line of a 17 week marathon that had started over four months earlier. As exhausted as he was, Wyland was excited about the opportunity to paint a mural in Key West.

"As soon as I saw the wall, I knew I wanted to paint Florida's living reef, the only living coral reef off the coast of the mainland United States," Wyland recalls. "Of course, I painted bottlenose dolphins in the mural, but I really wanted to focus on the reef so more people would be conscious of its beauty and perhaps become interested in helping to protect it."

Working with Reef Relief and many fine volunteers, the artist and his crew finished the mural and the entire East Coast Tour five minutes ahead of schedule.

The mural offers a window-like view into the underwater world of the Florida Keys, which Wyland feels was the perfect place to wrap up the grueling 17 city tour. "Key West is kind of like Hawaii — not too stressful," he says. "It was a good place to wind up."

Model for Sarasota wall

Whaling Wall LI — Sarasota, Florida — 45 feet long x 26 feet high — Dedicated September 20, 1993 by Michael Martin

Dedication crowd gathering

Painting green sea turtle

17 murals later

▲ **Whaling Wall LII** — Key West, Florida — 52 feet long x 45 feet high — Dedicated September 27, 1993 by Captain Tony

THE WEST COAST TOUR - SUMMER 1994...

WHALING WALL 53
ORCA'S OFF THE GULF OF MEXICO

The good people of South Padre Island, Texas, had been trying for three years to convince Wyland to paint a Whaling Wall in their community. The artist had yet to paint a mural along the Gulf Coast, and the warm nature of these South Texas people finally won him over. On March 7, 1994, he flew to the Lone Star State to paint his first mural since completing the marathon East Coast Whaling Wall Tour.

"It had been six months since the tour, and I was anxious to paint another Whaling Wall," Wyland recalls. "The people of South Padre Island were very enthusiastic and knowledgeable about the marine life in their waters. Plus, I had a chance to meet and work with Ila Loetscher, 'The Turtle Lady.'"

Wyland visited Ms. Loetscher, who, at age 90, is renowned for her work in helping to save the kemp's ridley turtle and other marine animals who have been stranded on Texas beaches.

Although a hard rain washed off most of the ocean background Wyland painted the first day, he started again the next morning and, by the end of the week, covered three sides of the Convention Center, with Gulf Coast marine life.

WHALING WALL 54
ALASKA'S MARINE LIFE

Wyland's West Coast Whaling Wall Tour kicked off on August 1, 1994, in Anchorage Alaska, the first stop on what would turn out to be 13 murals in eight cities in eight weeks.

"I arrived in Anchorage a few days early and had a chance to do some fishing and whale watching with Ron Morris of the National Marine Fishery" Wyland says.

"It was the perfect excursion to give me a first-hand look at the marine life in the area, and I knew immediately that I wanted to paint the bowhead whale and some belugas swimming near the ice packs in the Alaska fjords. I also added some spotted seals and a ribbon seal with her pup."

The 20-hour days of summertime Alaska allowed Wyland to paint late into the evening, and he finished the five-story, 400-foot mural in less than five days. "This was the first time I'd painted a Whaling Wall in Alaska, and the people of this city couldn't have been warmer," he says. "In fact, they reminded me so much of the people of Hawaii — high in spirit and full of aloha. I definitely want to return to Alaska one day and see how this mural looks when it's lighted, and maybe paint another wall in this great state."

It was a great start for Wyland and his team who migrated down the Pacific coast.

▲ Whaling Wall LIII — South Padre Island, Texas — 265 feet long x 25 feet high — Dedicated March 13, 1994 by project coordinator, Karen Moore

South Padre wall at dusk

Artist with belugas

Finishing Alaska wall

Painting bowhead's eye

▲ **Whaling Wall LIV** — Anchorage, Alaska — 400 feet long x 55 feet high — Dedicated August 8, 1994 by Mayor Rick Mystrom

WHALING WALL 55
ORCA'S A-30 SUBPOD

Vancouver, British Columbia, was high on the artist's list for the West Coast Tour because he would be able to paint a Whaling Wall at the renowned Vancouver Aquarium, directly across from the aquarium's orca tank. The other reason was that he would be working with Dr. John Ford, one of the most respected authorities on orca whales in the world.

"This Whaling Wall was extra special for me, not only because I got to work with John, but because I wanted to do something in the memory of a great marine biologist named Michael Bigg. Michael had worked with me on Whaling Wall 13 in 1987. He passed away several years ago, and it was an honor for me to dedicate the Vancouver Aquarium mural to him and his family."

Wyland painted an actual pod of orca whales that frequent the waters of Robson Bight. It was the A-30 subpod, which Wyland himself had dived with a couple of years earlier. The aquarium wall was only 15 feet high, but it was over a hundred feet long, enabling the artist to paint each of five whales detailed down to the individual scars and markings on their dorsal fins.

WHALING WALL 56
VANCOUVER ISLAND ORCAS

For ten years, Wyland had been looking at a wall in Vancouver that stood sentry beside the Granville Street Bridge. It is estimated that 70,000 cars a day pass over this bridge as they enter the downtown district of Vancouver. Thanks to Wyland's good friend David Green and city officials, the artist was given the green light to paint.

With one week scheduled in each city on the tour, Wyland finished the mural at the aquarium on Friday and moved over to the Granville site and went to work immediately. "I only had two days to finish this wall, which actually was two walls separated by a large section of windows that belonged to the rooms of a seven-story boarding house," he says. "It was quite a challenge, but once I got going, I knew I could do it."

The diptych mural allowed the artist to paint the sixth member of the A-30 subpod he'd just finished at the aquarium, tying the two Whaling Walls together thematically. It took Wyland only 12 hours to finish both sides of the mural. Now anyone driving into Vancouver from the Granville Street Bridge is welcomed by a life-size male orca breaching out of the misty waters of Robson Bight.

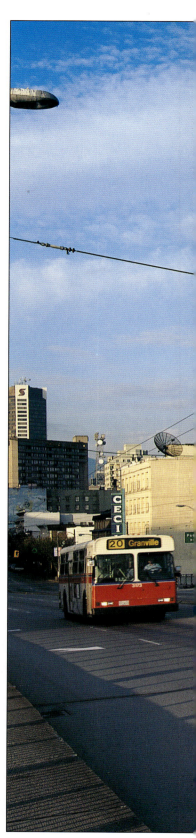

Whaling Wall LV — Vancouver, British Columbia, Canada — 185 feet long x 15 feet high — Dedicated August 15, 1994 by Dr. John Ford in memory of Mike Bigg

Detail of A-30 subpod

Wyland with Dr. John Ford and assistant

Beautiful view from Granville Bridge

▲ **Whaling Wall LVI** — Vancouver, British Columbia, Canada — 80 feet long x 90 feet high — Dedicated August 15, 1994 by Dr. John Ford

WHALING WALL 57
LEAP OF FAITH

The Whaling Wall Wyland had painted in Seattle in 1985, "The orcas of Puget Sound," had deteriorated due to its exposure to the elements and was painted over. Wyland, of course, had wanted for years to paint another mural in Seattle, and the West Coast Tour offered him the perfect opportunity.

"I'd painted sunset colors on canvas, but this was the first time I'd used these warm colors for a mural," he says. "This wall not only faced the famous Seattle Space Needle, where millions of people will be able to view it, but it was graced by what is called the "sweet light" of the late afternoon sun, just before it sets. I wanted this painting to reflect the peace and natural light of the environment in which this great orca lives, and I think I captured it. I'm very proud of this mural."

Govenor Mike Lowery dedicated the mural and proclaimed August 22, "Wyland Day" in the state.

WHALING WALL 58
ORCA'S OFF THE SAN JUAN ISLANDS

By finishing the first Seattle wall early, Wyland had the opportunity to take a sea-plane with some friends from the Friday Harbor Whale Museum to observe local killer whale pods near the San Juan Islands.

"We spotted a large group of orca whales and landed half a mile in front of the pod," he recalls. "To our amazement, 25 to 30 orcas headed straight for our sea-plane, some as close as 20 feet from the pontoons. To be able to go out and see these whales in their natural habitat is the ultimate first-hand experience for an artist."

Whaling Wall 58, depicts the J-1 pod, a local family of orca whales, and the two whales in the lower right corner are portraits of a baby orca (named after Dr. Michael Bigg) and its mother, both of whom were being filmed at the time for the movie "Free Willy II."

This wall was dedicated by Seattle Mayor, Norman Rice, who also went up on the scaffolding with Wyland and signed the mural at the Quality Inn.

▲ **Whaling Wall LVII** — Seattle, Washington — 45 feet long x 70 feet high — Dedicated August 22, 1994 by Govenor Mike Lowery

San Juan Island orca research

QVC Network features Wyland live at Seattle Wall

▲ **Whaling Wall LVIII** — Seattle, Washington — 45 feet long x 70 feet high — Dedicated August 22, 1994 by Mayor Norm Rice

WHALING WALL 59
GRAY WHALES OFF THE OREGON COAST

Newport, Oregon, was one of those small but phenomenally enthusiastic communities where everyone rolled out the red carpet for Wyland as he painted his 59th Whaling Wall.

The artist received additional inspiration when he and Dr. Bruce Mate, one of the top marine biologists in the world, were escorted by the U.S. Coast Guard in a Zodiac along the Oregon coastline. "We were encountering gray whales five minutes out of the jetty in Newport," Wyland says. "Then, on the second day, the actual mist settling over the Oregon coast was very much like I had envisioned it for the mural. Being directly exposed to all of my subjects and the environment I wanted to paint — I couldn't have asked for more."

During his trip with Dr. Mate, Wyland saw many gray whales that were year-round residents. "One of the local fishermen told me about a resident whale named "Scarback", and he provided me with a photo. Unfortunately, the picture revealed a huge scar from a harpoon wound the whale had suffered several years earlier. I was so moved by the story that I included Scarback in the mural. I try whenever I can to include actual living whales in my murals as a tribute to their individuality and biology."

WHALING WALL 60
SPYHOPPING GRAY WHALES

San Francisco's Pier 39, the fourth most visited attraction in California, draws over 12 million visitors each year, and with a brand-new aquarium under construction, the famous attraction presented a combination of visibility and aquatic theme that was perfect for Wyland's first Whaling Wall in the city.

Wyland actually had the opportunity to paint two murals at Pier 39, the first depicting two gray whales — a mother and calf — spyhopping off the coast of Northern California. San Francisco Mayor Frank Jordan, who proclaimed August 30 "Wyland Day," climbed aboard the scaffolding and helped paint a few barnacles with the artist. The mural is located across the street from Pier 39's entrance on the side of its five-story parking garage.

"Every car that drives along Fisherman's Wharf will see this wall," the artist says proudly. "By painting the two whales spyhopping, I wanted to educate the public as to this peculiar behavior and draw attention to the gray whale in celebration of its recent removal from the endangered species list."

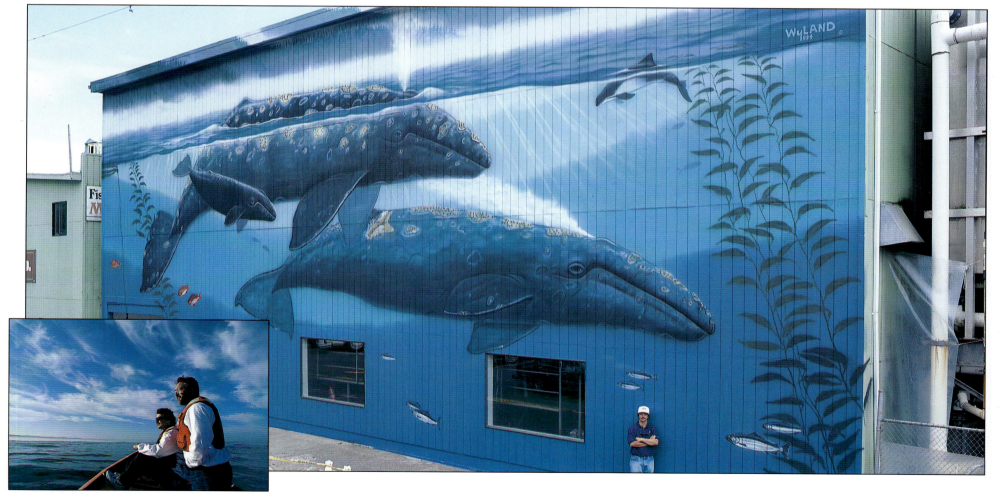

Wyland with whale researcher Dr. Bruce Mate

▲ **Whaling Wall LIX** — Newport, Oregon — 80 feet long x 32 feet high — Dedicated August 29, 1994 by Mayor Mark Collson and Dr. Bruce Mate

WHALING WALL 61
GRAYS OFF SAN FRANCISCO COAST

"The second wall at Pier 39 was smaller than the first one, but it was just as mighty," Wyland recalls. "It's right next to the entrance to the Pier so anyone who walks in can't possibly miss it. It'll also be situated next to the new aquarium the Pier is building, and we'll be printing a poster of the mural to raise funds for the Marine Mammal Center."

The actual design of the wall presented an interesting "angle" to this mural, as Wyland wrapped a gray whale around a slight bend in the middle of the wall. Also, because the mural was situated where the late afternoon sun hit the wall each day, the artist elected to use warm yellows and oranges for a beautiful sunset scene above the surface.

"This was only the second time I've used sunset colors for a Whaling Wall; the first time was in Seattle," Wyland explains. "When that sweet light from the afternoon sun spreads across the mural, the painting comes alive in a very natural way. It's as if the viewer and the whales are sharing the same sunset."

San Francisco wall at twilight

▲ **Whaling Wall LX** — San Francisco, California — 70 feet long x 25 feet high — Dedicated September 5, 1994 by Port Commissioner

▲ **Whaling Wall LXI** — San Francisco, California — 35 feet long x 55 feet high - Dedicated September 5, 1994 by Mayor Frank Jordan

WHALING WALL 62
CELEBRATING GRAY WHALES

When the West Coast Tour began, a site for a Whaling Wall in Los Angeles had yet to be determined. Soon, however, Wyland had contracts for the Paramount Studios' entrance, and the side of Mann's Chinese Theatre in Hollywood.

Wyland decided to paint the Chinese Theatre first, finishing the mural in three days amid a whirlwind media frenzy that included Entertainment Tonight, People Magazine, CNN, all three major network affiliates and other local, national and international press. On one day, over 11 television cameras were filming Wyland painting, with over 25 professional photographers clicking their shutters and 12 radio stations standing by for interviews.

"Having that kind of media attention was great because exposing as many people as I can to these murals is what this project is all about," Wyland says. "But, I have to be honest, it was hard to get any painting done. I'm surprised I finished the mural in time to move on to Paramount."

The Chinese Theatre is now able to offer millions of tourists and residents a new "drive-by" screen with a special feature attraction — three life-size gray whales and several dolphins playfully swimming in a bright green ocean.

Gray Whales on Hollywood Boulevard

Eye of the gray whale

Whaling in Hollywood

▲ **Whaling Wall LXII** — Los Angeles, California — 152 feet long x 37 feet high — Dedicated September 12, 1994 by Honorary Mayor of Hollywood, Johnny Grant

WHALING WALL 63
LIFE-SIZE BLUE WHALES

Immediately after finishing the Chinese Theatre wall, Wyland's spray guns and painting equipment were whisked over to the entrance of Paramount Studios. "I hadn't painted blue whales for a while, and I thought this would be a good opportunity to showcase just how beautiful and large they really are," he says. "Blue whales have made a tremendous comeback, and we're seeing many more of them off our coasts." Wyland set out to paint the adult female blue whale to be 100 feet long. When his team actually measured the completed whale, it was 97 feet long, and they estimated it to be approximately 200 tons in weight.

"Despite all of the excitement these walls created in Hollywood, my favorite part of the whole week in Los Angeles was when a class of children came over to the Paramount wall during the dedication ceremony," Wyland remembers with a smile. "It's certainly my intention to reach as many people as I can and draw attention to the ocean. But it's the kids who are the most important. They'll be the ones who'll inherit the responsibility of protecting our planet, and maybe the Whaling Walls will, in some small way, start them along this path of consciousness."

Celebrating blue whales

▲ Whaling Wall LXIII — Los Angeles California — 180 feet long x 85 feet high — Dedicated September 12, 1994 by Don "The Dragon" Wilson

WHALING WALL 64
SAN DIEGO MIGRATION

"This wall presented a very interesting canvas because it was very large, and it was separated into three parts by two long vertical strips of marble," Wyland says of the side of the San Diego National Bank. "I'd noticed previously that you can see this wall very clearly from the freeway and from the planes that fly in and out of San Diego International Airport. Once it's lighted, I think it'll be one of the most beautiful murals I've ever done."

The mural depicts five gray whales migrating down the coast of California on their way to Mexico, along with a sheepshead, some garabaldi and some tuna. Although he wanted to paint a number of gray whales during his West Coast Tour to celebrate their being removed from the endangered species list, Wyland expressed some concern about their habitat.

"The Mexican government is now considering building the largest salt mine in the world in the San Ignacio Lagoons, where thousands of gray whales migrate each year to mate and calve," he says. "I hope this mural will draw attention to these creatures, and move everyone who sees it to get involved in whatever way they can to encourage the government not to ruin this extremely important habitat. It doesn't make sense to bring whales back from extinction and then destroy where they live."

WHALING WALL 65
FRIENDLY GRAYS OFF SAN IGNACIO

The National University Science Museum was host to Wyland's first whaling wall in Mexico. Home to the great Mexican masters, Wyland's mural would be an historic first by any foreigner. "I was very anxious to share my art with the students at the University and create public art and awareness that is critical to the gray whale," said Wyland.

As the national media watched Wyland transform an otherwise boring wall into a split level view of San Ignacio Lagoon featuring a 55 foot gray whale and her calf. "In 1983 I visited the friendly gray whales in San Ignacio. As we entered the lagoon a group of grays followed our small skiff into the shallow water. A mother whale pushed her calf right up along side us so I could reach out and touch it," remembers Wyland.

Today I reflect that special place in this important mural with the hope that it will make an impact on the people of Mexico.

West Coast Tour crew - Team Wyland pod

▲ **Whaling Wall LXIV** — San Diego, California — 164 feet long x 80 feet high — Dedicated September 12, 1994 by Mayor Susan Golding

WHALING WALL 66
FREE KEIKO

The last mural on the tour would be the most special for the artist. The Reino Aventura Park in Mexico City agreed to release Keiko - Free Willy with the painting of Wyland's historic Whaling Wall mural. To date no one had secured the release of the 16 year old orca, and Wyland felt he could help in the release of this special whale to a rehabilitation facility and better environment. After meeting Keiko in June, Wyland spent two days diving with Keiko in some human orca bonding, before painting Keiko swimming free with a family of orcas at the parks entrance.

"It is a great honor to have Keiko as a friend and I look forward to working with the Reino Aventura people to the day when Keiko will swim free again," said Wyland.

Wyland with Keiko

▲ Whaling Wall LXV — Mexico City, Mexico — 85 feet long x 20 feet high — Dedicated September 26, 1994 by Dr. Jorge Flores Valdes
▲ Whaling Wall LXVI — Mexico City, Mexico — 200 feet long x 45 feet high — Dedicated September 26, 1994 by Alejandro Azcue Carrillo

VII
PAINTING GIANT MURALS

...If you don't make any mistakes, it doesn't take long at all...

▲ Painting life-size Atlantic right whale, Atlantic, GA 1993

I've always enjoyed the challenge of painting large murals. I simply try not to think of the overall scale. To me, it is just painting a very large picture. I work very much the same way when I do an oil painting. The best way to explain how I paint is to envision a giant Polaroid photograph developing before your eyes. In other words, a mass of color slowly coming into sharp focus. I generally prepare each wall by pressure-washing the surface, after which a two-part epoxy primer sealer is either sprayed or rolled on. Each wall can be measured, and the overall square footage can be estimated to determine how much paint is needed to complete the various stages of the mural. After the initial priming of the wall, I start by painting different bands of colors. I first try to get an overall visual of how large the surface is in my mind's eye. I then proceed with an industrial, airless spray gun to cover the entire background with bands of color until the entire wall is completely covered with paint. At first, my murals look like big mistakes. It looks like an artist ran out of one color and had to use another. At this point, it's very hard to imagine what the mural will look like at completion. I've found that I need to be thick-skinned. In an artist's studio, the public would never see an unfinished canvas, or dirty laundry as we call it. But, when you're painting giant murals, your every move is under the watchful eye of the public. Fortunately, I've painted so many

Blank wall

Preparing wall

Priming wall

145

Painting background colors

Painting orca whales

Finished mural six weeks later

▲ Whaling Wall 33 aerial view, Long Beach, CA

Day 1 - September 7, 1993

Press conference with Atlanta Mayor, Maynard Jackson

Team Wyland pep talk

Roy and Wyland prepare airless spray gun

murals that I have a good idea of the progress of the mural. I generally know if it is going to be good when the first bands of color are sprayed on the wall.

First, I paint the entire ocean or environment. Once the environment is painted across the wall, I then look into that body and visualize whales and other marine life swimming onto the wall and paint them one at a time.

Traditionally, large murals were done with a lot of preliminary drawing and grids. Michelangelo would draw each section of the mural on paper and then pinpoint all the lines. They would then be chalked onto the wall to be sure it was accurate. Fortunately for me, I've been blessed with a talent to paint on a large scale without having to use any grids or preliminary sketches. I work entirely from my mind's eye. While I'm standing on the scaffolding, in close proximity to the wall, my mind's eye is several blocks away looking at the entire mural. It is similar to an out-of-body experience. I've found that with each mural, it has become increasingly easier to work on this scale. I've spent many years studying my subjects in their natural habitat and have painted them for many years in my studio. I've also reviewed a large library of films and books, and I refer to them mentally when I start painting the animals on the wall. The years of study have allowed me to paint these giant animals quite effortlessly.

Painting first right whale

Painting mural details

Finishing last whale

Painting first background colors

Bands of ocean colors

Finishing background colors

Most muralists I've met or read about, such as one of my favorite contemporary muralists, Kent Twichell, actually grid off every square foot of the mural to assure the accuracy. I'm sure that if I owned the building, I would probably do the same thing, but my philosophy is, what the heck, it's not my wall. . . just paint it.

My tools are very untraditional. Having been born in Detroit, I find it ironic that my murals are painted with automotive spray guns. The largest spray gun I use to paint most of the background colors is an airless spray gun. This gun allows me to cover the entire wall in a very short period of time. After I've covered the wall with paint, the next step is to start painting in sharper details. For this step, I use an automotive spray gun. It is a standard spray gun to paint cars. It works well for me because I can change colors in the cup rapidly, and I can achieve anywhere from a 12-inch spray area to a fine half-inch sharp line. I can also control the air pressure to create different effects. Most of my murals are completed using these two tools, along with some smaller paint brushes used in fine detailing. In the past, I've also used various natural sponges, but spray guns are my primary tools for large murals. I've discovered over the years that the air brush I used in my early days was too small. My philosophy is: less is more. It's preferable to me to paint an entire mural with one or two spray guns, and one or two brushes.

As far as paint goes, I use blues, greens, black,

Day 6 - September 12, 1993 Finished

Finished mural

Birds-eye view of Atlanta's Whaling Wall

Celebrating 50 Whaling Walls

white, red and yellow as my primary colors. At each mural site, I have a designated area called my "kitchen," where I keep all my equipment and mix paint. In the kitchen, I pick and choose all the colors for the mural. The colors are determined by the particular scene I'm depicting. For instance, if I'm in Hawaii and painting the Pacific Ocean, the colors of the sky and water are more vibrant. A mural in the Pacific Northwest, however, would reflect subtle colors and the spirit of that environment.

    When I paint, I try not to think. It slows me down. I basically feel it and transfer it to the wall. If I'm painting the sky, I look at the sky and mix the colors accordingly. The best thing I can do in painting a mural is to camouflage the fact that it is a large, ugly wall. My ultimate goal is to have the mural blend with the natural surrounding environment.

    It's ironic that I'm terrified of heights. In painting these murals, I've been up as high as 20 stories above the ground so I try not to think about the height or falling when I'm up on the scaffolding. Most of the scaffolding I used in the early days was the type that piled one upon the other. Today, what I use is much more sophisticated. For the taller buildings, I use a sky climber or swing stage. The scaffolding is on heavy cables, and motors lift the scaffolding up to the top of the building. Sometimes the murals require several if not dozens of scaffolds. I jump from one to the other to complete the mural. If the wall is not too high, I like using a cherry picker. I have someone drive it along the wall while I paint. It allows me to paint quickly, and I can move to any spot on the wall, both vertically and horizontally.

    Painting giant murals is no big thing — you just have to have big brushes and lots of paint!

Wyland is a phenomenon, a Johnny Appleseed covering the land with his oceans and whales. He reminds me of the days of barnstorming and circuses coming to town. He's the daredevil going over Niagara Falls in a barrel or walking a tightrope between skyscrapers. He brings back a spirit that's been somehow missing, a uniquely American entrepreneurial celebration of freedom and possibilities and endless afternoons of realizing dreams.

- Kent Twitchell

First day, background colors

Bands of color

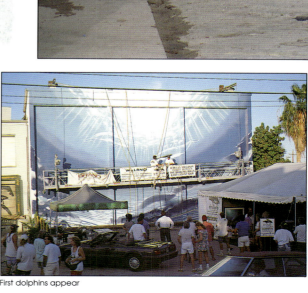
First dolphins appear

Mural sharpens

Final details

Dive in!

▲ Whaling Wall 52, Key West, FL

Day 1, June 15, 1993

Blank wall

First sky colors

Painting breaching whale

Above water completed

Checking mural progress

Background completed

Ghosting in mother and calf

Finishing mother and calf

Day 3, June 17, 1993

Finished Boston mural

VIII
DIVING WITH WHALES

...When you see a whale, you become a changed person...

▲ Artist diving with friendly humpback whale

Maui research

E ver since I saw Jacques Cousteau's specials in the early '70s, I've wanted to dive with whales. The romance and idea that one could experience diving next to the greatest creatures on earth was something I thought could only happen on television or in a fairy tale. But later, after moving to Maui in 1980, I was about to live one of my dreams.

Having studied and painted whales for years, I've seen the way they normally behave in their natural habitats. But the whales that migrated along the California coast, on their way to the lagoons of San Ignacio, Mexico, where they mate and give birth each winter, gave me a chance to view many of their behaviors. I've seen them breaching (when they jump clear out of the water — up to their tail flukes.) I've seen whales spyhopping (sticking their heads and eyes out of the water to have a look around). I've seen pods of orca whales off of Vancouver Island. And I've seen numerous whales above the water. But, I've always dreamed of

Humpback surfacing

Wyland swimming with Atlantic bottlenose dolphins

...If the oceans are calling, it must be the song of the whales...

Barnacle encrusted gray whale

Spyhopping gray whale, San Ignacio Lagoon, MX

Touching friendly gray whale

Gray whale fluke

swimming with them and, as an artist, experiencing their world, a world where few have ever ventured. Jacques Cousteau was my hero, and he had swum with the great whales. Of course, I wanted my own experience with them, not only to satisfy my curiosity, but also to assure me that my paintings were as accurate as possible.

When you see whales, you usually only see a small portion of their bodies above the water, like icebergs. I felt very strongly that if I could show these animals above and below the surface, more people would become aware of their unique size and beauty. I wanted to share my vision with others who may never have the opportunity to see these animals. So, it was necessary for me to swim with them.

As I began to study these creatures, I began to appreciate how rare it is to have an encounter with one of them. The truth is that you only see whales if they want you to. Not only do you have to be in the right place at the right time, but the whale has to agree to the encounter. These animals are so adapted to being unseen and avoiding human contact that they are sometimes impossible to detect and view. I truly believe that in the past few hundred years, having been constantly hunted, the whales have developed a communication system with each other to avoid the dangers of man.

In recent years, however, whales have, for some reason, made efforts to show themselves to us. I believe they're intelligent and sensitive, and they know instinctively when to appear. This is an amazing fact.

Swimming with whales has impacted my work more than any other event. To be able to swim under the ocean and view humpback whales, for instance, has changed forever the way I paint them on canvas and in murals. I was awed by the complete control these giant animals had swimming in their environment. They were as graceful as any ballerina. I immediately sensed, as I entered their world, that these animals knew I was there to help them. They cautiously approached me and allowed me to view them in their natural habitat. Talk about an artist's model!

A mother humpback swimming with her calf once studied *me*. We made direct eye contact. I knew as I looked into her eye that I was looking into the soul of an ancient being. This was an intelligent, beautiful animal that has evolved for over 40 million years on this ocean planet. In my excitement, as I swam up to the animal, I almost forgot to breathe. I had to surface. When I dove again, I didn't realize how close I was to the whale. She had to lift her flipper over my head to avoid colliding with me. To my amazement, the whales did not flee; they stayed with us for what seemed to be a very long time. Near the mother and calf was an escort whale, whom I'd studied for many years. This first experience of diving with the humpbacks off Maui is still reflected in my paintings, sculptures and life-size murals.

Since that time, I have had the unique opportunity to dive with whales, dolphins and other marine life all over the world. In fact, I consider that to be the best part of my job. This is really a hobby that turned into a career. Over the years, I've found that my murals seem to be a rallying point for people concerned about whales, dolphins and the ocean. Fortunately for me, I have met many groups and individuals who are concerned about these animals and have also invited me to be part of their ongoing whale studies.

I've had many encounters with various marine mammals. Dolphins are a favorite of mine. I've admired them since watching *Flipper* on television. Swimming with them has been another youthful fantasy, and I've enjoyed swimming with them in many different areas of the world.

I find dolphins to be intelligent, beautiful, unique and individual, as we are. Like whales, they have specific features and personalities that identify them as individuals. The more time I spend swimming and studying them, I have a greater appreciation for what makes them unique. Some of them have overbites, and others have underbites. Some are shy, others are curious and others are friendly. Some will swim right over to you. It's a very special experience that I try to imitate on canvas.

I don't want to over-personify whales and dolphins, but sometimes it's impossible. Some of them remind me of people I've met, and some of them even look like people I know. These animals are very

Humpback whale breaching

Dear Wyland,

In the early 1980's we met a young and talented artist who shared our concern for the great whales of our planet. Little did we know then, that this artist's zeal and compassion for our brothers the whales, would make such an impact on how we humans see the world in which we live. Through his work, and in particular, his incredible mastery of large, or rather "huge" murals, he has been able to strike our collective consciousness with the truth of knowledge. As we work on the ocean day in and day out, trying to better understand the humpback whale and their critical needs, it is gratifying to know that there is someone out there who has captured the spirit of the whales. He portrays them as "life-size" so that all of us might share their magnificence, and work so diligently at educating "man-kind" to the other wonders of life we share with all living things. We are pleased to say thank you ("mahalo") for your good will ("kokua") dear friend, Wyland. Thank you for your help, thank you for your talent, and thank you for the "whales"!

Mark J. Ferrari

Deborah Glockner-Ferrari

special and worthy of protection.

A very special place for me is the Pacific Northwest, where orca whales are abundant. I've had the opportunity to dive with some of the local pods. There are two reasons someone will dive with killer whales: insanity and curiosity. When I swam with

Whale watching

the orcas, I was banking on the fact that they fed exclusively on local salmon and not marine mammals or sea lions. I definitely was not going to wear the seal suit to find out.

Over the past 10 years, I've been fortunate enough to be part of a research team in Maui, studying the humpback whales each winter from January until May. I've also experienced sperm whales off the Hawaiian Islands. They're huge! Some are larger than 60 feet! I've seen pilot whales, false killer whales, killer whales, gray whales, beluga whales, minke whales, finback whales, harbor porpoises and spotted dolphins. And I've had the opportunity to swim with many of them. Some of the larger whales we've been swimming with have generally been just "hanging out" with dolphins and pilot whales. They are, after all, related, being members of the same cetacean family.

The songs of the whales are beautiful and haunting. Each year, the song is a little longer and different. These songs, which travel many miles underwater, are in stereo and are unforgettable. To me, humpbacks sound like cows and birds. There's nothing comparable to swimming with whales and seeing and hearing them as they live and breathe.

I also enjoy swimming with other marine life. I've had many shark encounters over the years and have swum with makos, blues, white tips, tiger sharks and hammerheads. Another favorite underwater animal is the sea turtle. They move through the water with grace and command. I've also seen sea lions, elephant seals, sea otters, barracudas and manta rays. Once, when we were swimming in Molokini crater, we saw a 17 foot manta ray that resembled a dinosaur.

I enjoy diving as a sport, and to be able to dive with whales and dolphins is the ultimate. Native people say that being eye to eye with an eagle is the highest. I understand what they mean because for me, to be eye to eye with a humpback whale is the epitome of spirituality. I hope to share this experience through my art.

Underwater right whale

Sperm whale sighting

Right whale and calf

photos by Iain Kerr - Whale Conservation Institute

▲ Wyland diving with green sea turtles

Wyland observing pilot whales, Japan

Pilot whale

Right whale sunset

IX
ORIGINAL PAINTINGS

161

...Everyone always asks how long it takes me to complete a painting...I say this year it took 37 years...Next year 38...

▲ Another Day at the Office — Oil by Wyland, Warren 36" x 48" ©1994

HANAUMA BAY

For many years, I have experienced Oahu's Hanauma Bay, a marine sanctuary and one of Hawaii's premier tourist attractions. However, the problem with Hanauma Bay is that it has become *too* popular. At one point it was estimated that over 40,000 people per day were impacting this unique marine habitat. But recently, in an effort to save it, the state of Hawaii has worked to limit access to the bay to 5,000 visitors a day.

I was approached by The University of Hawaii to do an original painting to raise funds and awareness of the bay's unique marine life. This painting took me over a month to complete. First, I went down to the bay and photographed it from different angles. Then, I went back to my studio and did a split level view both above and below the water. I feel this painting will do much to create a greater awareness to the many beautiful creatures that make Hanauma Bay their home.

Visiting Hanauma Bay, HI

▲ Hanauma Bay — Oil 4' x 6' ©1993

...Man's desire to use the oceans without regard to leaving it as he found it may destroy the very beauty he came to see...

GRAY WHALE WATERS

Each year, Dana Point celebrates its annual Festival of the Whales. This past year, I was asked to create the official painting for the festival, which celebrates the migration of the California gray whale. This painting is an original watercolor.

For me, painting whales and other marine life with water seems to be the most natural. Although I've painted many watercolors over the years, *Gray Whale Waters* is the first original painting I had published in a limited edition print and a fine art poster. Watercolor has a look unto itself. I work very wet when I use this medium. In fact, most of the paint drips off the watercolor paper onto the floor. But what is left on the paper when it dries is a texture that looks like real barnacles and real whale skin. I also like the way the water falls off the paper with the many abstract shapes that are achieved. This is a spontaneous process. Watercolor remains the most challenging of all painting mediums, but it's also one of the most rewarding.

FIRST BREATH

First Breath was the only painting I finished on my 1993 East Coast tour. I had the good fortune of painting a smaller mural at the National Zoo in Washington, D.C., which allowed me the time to paint an oil painting. Due to the fact that the wall was much smaller, I had a window of time. Because I love to paint, I visited an art store in D.C. and bought a lot of art supplies just so I could do this one painting. I'd been thinking about this painting for a number of years and had already done a bronze sculpture of *First Breath*. When an image comes to me, I become obsessed to paint it, and this one actually painted itself. I painted it at the National Zoo's auditorium in front of several hundred people. When it was completed, I knew I had a winner. I was so happy with this painting that I offered the entire limited edition lithograph to the Very Special Arts in Washington, D.C. This is a group of artists with disabilities. Luckily, the group had come to the zoo and watched *First Breath* being painted for them. These limited editions will help fund the Very Special Arts programs on a national level.

The painting depicts a mother whale helping her calf to the surface for its first breath. The Smithsonian Institute expressed interest in keeping the painting for their permanent exhibit, but it's one of those paintings I want to keep for myself. Maybe I'll donate it to the Smithsonian in the future, but for now, it remains in my private collection.

▲ Gray Whale Waters — Watercolor 15" x 23" ©1992

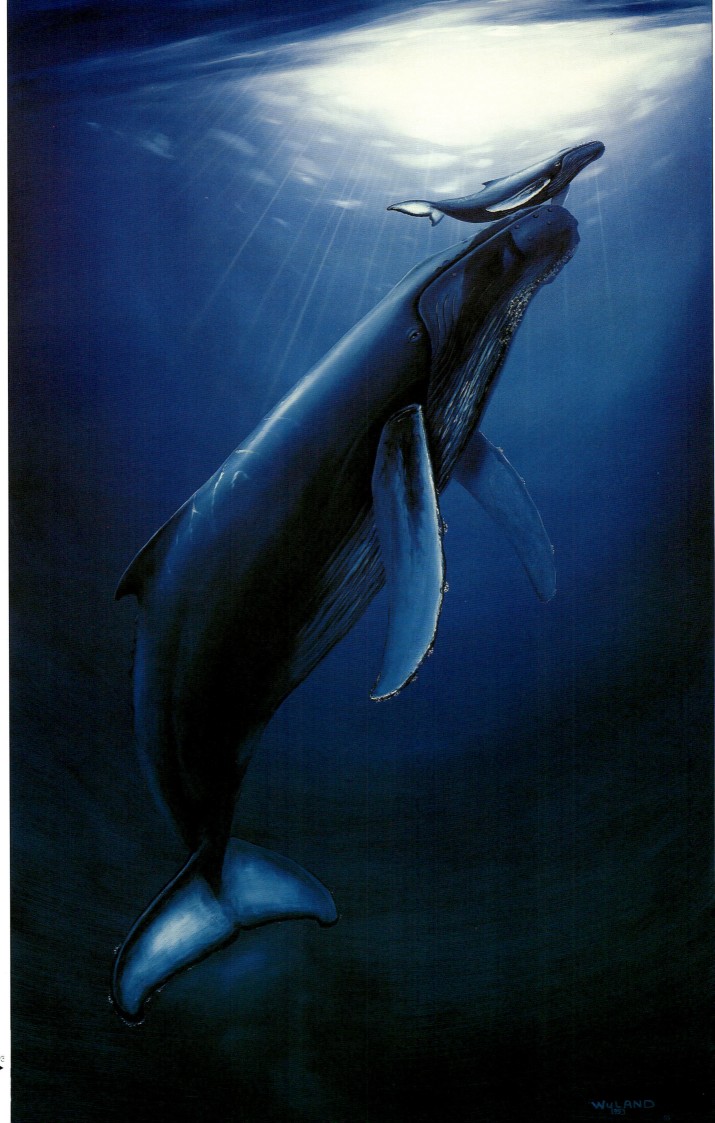

First Breath - Oil 48" x 72" ©1993

DOLPHIN VISION

Dolphin Vision actually evolved after the East Coast tour when I had the opportunity to dive off of St. Lucia and Bonaire. I was experimenting with a new underwater camera — a Nikonas RS. I've been taking underwater photographs with a Nikonas camera for many years, but this new camera was very appealing. It had a lot of unique features. I wanted to somehow take a photo, blow it up into a large cibachrome and then paint onto that print to make the perfect picture. This was a collaboration of my photography and my original painting. So, we now call it underwater photography painting.

As an underwater photographer, you usually can only wish for a dolphin to swim right in front of your lens at the perfect time with the perfect light. This time, it happened for me. And it was a tremendous opportunity for me to capture the spirit of what I envision underwater and the spirit of what I can create in my painting studio.

Dolphin Vision is the first of a series of underwater photography paintings I hope to complete each year as I continue to dive and photograph the oceans of the world. What's interesting about this painting is that the viewer cannot tell where the painting starts and the photograph ends. To my surprise, when I got the transparencies back from the lab, the smaller fish I'd painted in many of my paintings over the last 15 years were there in the photograph. For years I had remarked to others that I'd seen these fish. Everyone always wanted to know what kind of fish they were. I would say that they were Cousteau fish. If you watch a Cousteau special, you always see them. But there they were in the photograph. People who see them think I painted them. And, if you look closely, you'll also see what looks like a mermaid tail.

Wyland photographing undersea life

...The first artist was God. He's still the best...

▲ Dolphin Vision — Oil and Cibachrome 40" x 60" ©1994

ABOVE AND BELOW

Wyland with Robert Bateman Victoria, B.C.

In 1935, at a ceremony dedication of Wylands Whaling Wall thirteen in Victoria, British Columbia, acclaimed wildlife artist Robert Bateman looked up at the American artist's life size mural depicting a pod of thirteen orca whales and stared, "I believe I see a bald eagle up there. I thought we had an agreement, you would paint below the ocean and I was supposed to do above." With this idea emerged the concept of two artists creating a single painting.

Several years later, Wyland mentioned the idea to a friend Roy Tabora, Hawaii's foremost seascape painter.

THE BEST OF TWO WORLDS

Together Wyland and Roy pioneered the Above and Below series. To date Wyland has collaborated with renowned artists Roy Gonzalez Tabora, James Coleman, Tracy Taylor, Jim Warren and John Pitre. Wyland continues to explore new frontiers in fine art collaborations with leading artists throughout the world. "The Above and Below Series has brought artists together to create the best of two worlds."

Wyland and Tabora in Hawaii studio

▲ Ocean Trilogy — Oil by Wyland/Tabora 24" x 64" triptych ©1993

▲ Whale Waters — Oil by Wyland/Tabora 48" round © 1992

ROY GONZALEZ TABORA

Roy Gonzalez Tabora was destined to be an artist. Born into a family of painters in 1956, young Tabora was brought up in a world where art was a way of life. Under the watchful eye of a loving uncle, his hand was skillfully trained to reproduce what his heart saw. Those early days as a studio apprentice fueled his desire to elevate his art to one day stand among the works of the finest, past and present. By the age of twenty, the years of training and discipline had produced a highly accomplished realist painter. His quest for excellence continued with a formal education in fine art from the University of Hawaii. Today he is recognized as one of the world's leading seascape painters.

The breathtaking splendor and consummate artistry of his work speaks for itself. Nature alone is the subject of Tabora's work. The compelling beauty of Hawaii's majestic shores provide a never-ending source of inspiration. Each new canvas becomes a masterpiece of harmony as memory and imagination fuse; a dynamic interplay of land and sky and sea, bathed in radiant light.

JAMES COLEMAN

Coleman's career, spanning 22 years, has made him one of Walt Disney Productions' most important artists. A master of color and light, Coleman fills each of his creations with an energy and mood only nature itself can surpass. Although he is continually sought after today for motion picture work, Coleman spends the majority of his time painting and is represented by some of the most prominent galleries in North America and the Hawaiian Islands. Coleman's pieces have become a part of many significant personal and corporate collections including the Disney family's. His work has been displayed at the Metropolitan Museum of Art and in traveling exhibits both in the U.S. and abroad. Coleman had been a finalist for four consecutive years in the Art for the Parks competition. His paintings are part of a permanent catalogue and traveling exhibition for this contest, which is hosted by the National Parks System every year. Coleman's radiant landscapes are recognized as important contributions to both film and fine art, making his artwork highly valued by collectors all over the world.

Pitre, Tabora, Wyland, Coleman

Coleman and Wyland, Hawaii

Belugas
Oil by Wyland/Coleman
4' × 5' ©1993

TRACY TAYLOR

Tracy Taylor paints seahorses, mermaids, pirate's treasure, and miles and smiles of marvelous, magical fish. A self-taught watercolorist and veteran kid-at-heart, she paints playfully and effortlessly, captivating viewers with her colorful tropical renditions. Tracy's refreshing and uninhibited technique makes her work ever-popular with old and young alike; especially appealing are her vibrant colors and humorous titles. Her prize-winning style is eagerly sought out. Much of her time is devoted to keeping up with the demand of private watercolor commissions and ongoing nationwide gallery exhibitions. Aside from her painting, Tracy takes pleasure in raising her children, relishing in a good game of pool and her new found hobby of scuba diving.

Hi! I'm Tracy Taylor. I'm a friend of Wyland's. In October, I saw Wyland at the Art Expo in Los Angeles. He said, "Tracy, let's do a collaboration." I wish I could remember the restaurant that we went to shoot pool. Three days later, I flew down to his studio in Laguna. We worked hard and had a great time. I like to paint in the morning, he likes to paint at night. I know iced tea is his favorite beverage. I never had my picture taken so much in my entire life. It was fun working with a famous artist. At one point Wyland said, " It's amazing we can both fit in the same room." We laughed a lot. The artistic ego. I hope you enjoy the pieces - it's obvious we did. Thank you for your continued support.

Wyland and Tracy Taylor, Wyland studio, Laguna Beach

Who Invited These Guys? — Watercolor by Wyland/Taylor 40" x 60" © 1993

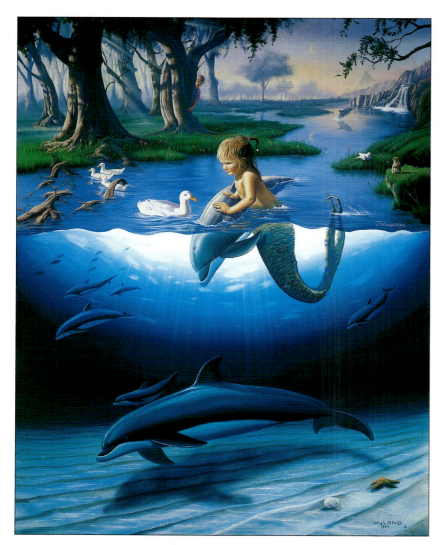

JIM WARREN

Jim Warren's unique style is in fact something of a cross between Salvador Dali's surrealism and Norman Rockwell's Americana Illustration style.

Jim Warren is a lifelong resident of Long Beach, California where he resides with his wife Cindy, their baby daughter Drew and son, Art.

His work first caught the attention of the press and public when he won 1st place at the prestigious Westwood, California Art Show in 1975. He won two additional first place ribbons at two subsequent Westwood Art Shows. A few years later, a painting he produced for the cover of Bob Seger's album

"Against the Wind," won a Grammy Award in 1988 for "Best Album package (cover)." Jim has continued to earn many awards and acknowledgments for the quality of his work over a painting career spanning almost 2 decades. His most recent award was the "Judge's Choice" ribbon at the Luncheon Art Show in New York City, in March of 1992.

Jim's art has appeared on hundreds of book covers, album covers and movie posters over the years.

JOHN PITRE

John Pitre was born in 1942 and educated in the fine arts at the Art Students League in New York City. He evolved to become America's leading surrealist and social commentary painter, selling more prints world wide than any other artist. Pitre gained extraordinary popularity during the '60s and '70s painting daring themes such as over population, the threat of drugs and the ecological deterioration of our planet well before they became the obvious problems of our times. His social commentary paintings are now considered twentieth century classics, sought after by prominent collectors worldwide.

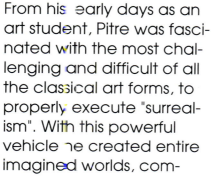

From his early days as an art student, Pitre was fascinated with the most challenging and difficult of all the classical art forms, to properly execute "surrealism". With this powerful vehicle he created entire imagined worlds, completely from his mind, evoking emotion and response in his viewers more so than with any other medium.

▲ Littlest Mermaid — Oil by Wyland/Warren 36" x 48" © 1993

▲ Aumakua and the Ancient Voyagers — Oil by Wyland/Pitre 18" x 25" ©1992
▶ Whale Rides — Oil by Wyland/Warren 18" x 26" ©1993

175

X
SCULPTURE

...I consider myself a sculptor who paints...

▲ Finishing Synchronicity bronze sculpture at Maiden Foundry, Portland, OR

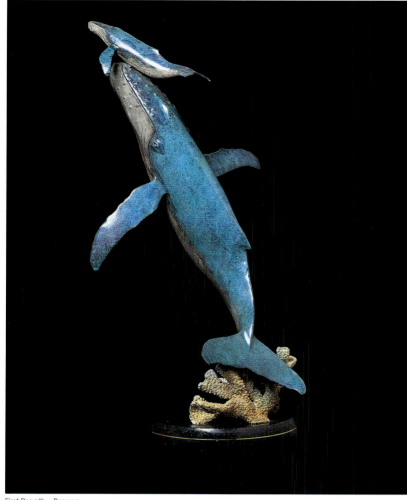
First Breath - Bronze

Wyland at sculpture studio

I've always felt I was a better sculptor than painter. Making sculpture for me began early, when an art teacher in elementary school threw down a lump of brown clay on my table in art class. To my surprise, I found shaping clay into figures and animals as natural as drawing and painting.

Years later, I would major in sculpture at the prestigious Center for Creative Studies, formerly the Society for Creative Studies in Detroit, Michigan. At that time, we were disciplined in sculpting the human form exclusively from live models. My teacher, Jay Holland, was very passionate about sculpture and inspired us to study, observe and measure the human anatomy, with particular focus on proportions. After two years, we completed one-third, one-half and full-scale figures.

This early foundation at the Center for Creative Studies helped me to later pay attention to anatomical detail when I began sculpting my first whales and dolphins. These days, of course, my marine models seldom hold still. But they do sometimes share a few precious minutes of their time which I hope to capture later in wax or clay.

Most of my sculpture starts with a drawing. Many years of diving

Great White - Bronze

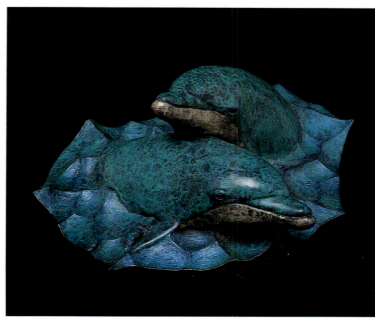
Dolphin Love - Bronze

Ocean Travelers - Bronze

180

Marlin - Bronze

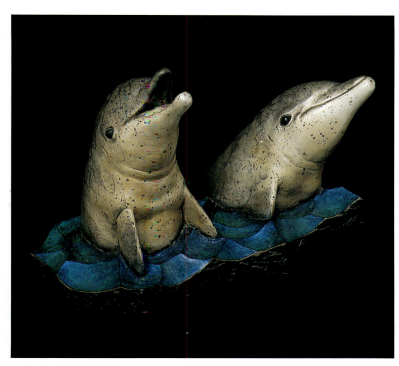

Friends of the Sea - Bronze

Gray whales - Bronze

with marine mammals and extensive research allow me to see the living sculpture in my mind's eye. As the whales and dolphins move through their ocean world, I try to record images that will later be reflected in my work. My ultimate goal is to capture forever in sculpture a single moment in time that shares the unique beauty these great animals possess.

Today, I have created a series of bronze sculpture featuring humpback whales, orcas, gray whales, belugas, dolphins, turtles, sharks, sea otters, manta rays and billfish for enthusiastic collectors around the world.

I feel very fortunate to be able to work with the Maiden Foundry in Sandy, Oregon. The artist and foundry must work together closely to develop an original finished bronze that conveys the artist's style and signature of the highest quality. After I've completed the original sculpture, it then goes through months of foundry work, including moldmaking, wax replicas, spruing, investment, de-waxing, casting, welding, finishing and finally, the patina finish.

Swimming with beluga whale

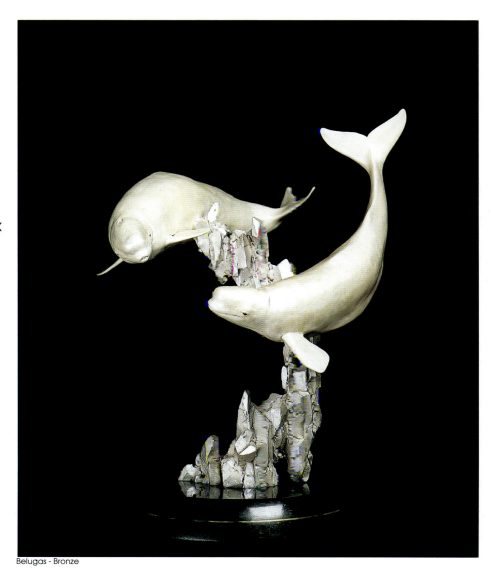

Belugas - Bronze

182

Kissing Dolphins - Acrylic

ACRYLIC

A new medium for me is a series of acrylic sculpture. Several years ago, I met Paul Killian, who invented a new acrylic sculpture that reflects an inner light that can only be achieved through this space-age medium. These translucent sculpture are the first of their kind, reflecting many different variations of color, form and dimension when receiving both natural and artificial light. The light literally radiates from these pieces.

Friends of the Sea - Acrylic

Whale Tail - Acrylic

SCULPTURE

I've noticed recently that my sculpture keep getting bigger. Again, I'm feeling the desire to create these majestic creatures in their true size. Just as artists throughout history have produced monumental sculpture of great figures, I now have the opportunity to create, for the first time, a giant series of marine art fountains, integrating public art, the environment, science and the sensation of being in the presence of one of God's greatest creations.

Dolphin Family - Acrylic

Great White - Acrylic

Marlin - Acrylic

▲ "Spouty" - Spouting off about the environment

XI
CHILDREN'S GALLERY

...If one kid grows up to be another Cousteau, all my efforts will have been worthwhile..

▲ Mote Marine Laboratory - Children's contest, Sarasota, FL

Over the years, I've experienced the fantastic art of many children. It's most gratifying to meet kids when I'm painting Whaling Walls. Often, they're inspired to create their own works of art on a smaller scale, but with equal emotion. Many of these kids are concerned about the ocean, whales and dolphins, and they want to help. I'm always excited to see the kids expressing their uninhibited imagination through art. Some of them are better artists than I was at their age. I sometimes find myself looking over my shoulder as I paint these walls. Some of these kids are incredible! I hope my art will, in some small way, inspire them to continue on the path of consciousness as opposed to convenience. I will then feel that all my efforts will have been worthwhile. I said once that if one of these kids grows up to be another Cousteau, then it will be a great achievement for me. As I was painting one of my walls, one kid hollered, "What about another Wyland?" All I could do was smile.

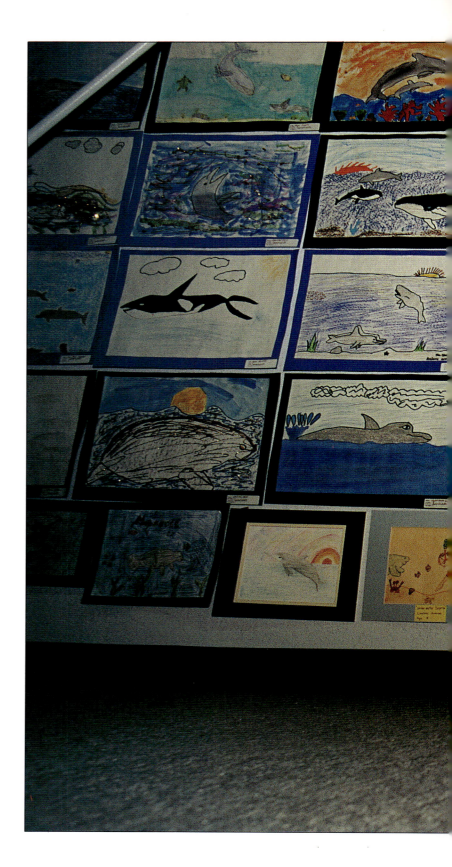

Wyland's ocean art winners

...Clean water and a healthy ocean are important to everyone...

▲ Wyland in an ocean of children's art, Mote Marine Laboratory, Sarasota, FL

XII
VISION

...Today we celebrate living whales...

▲ Two Worlds of Paradise — Oil by Wyland ~ Walfrido 3' X 4' ©1994

For me, I feel I can make my biggest impact with the children — for future generations. Fortunately, I have a unique opportunity to reach tens of thousands of kids via the Whaling Walls. Last summer on my East Coast tour, I talked to groups of kids in 17 different cities, totaling over 70,000 children in a little over four months. Fortunately, I've painted Whaling Walls for over 13 years, long enough that I've been able to see the impact my work has had on various people. A month doesn't pass when I don't get a letter telling me that one of my Whaling Walls has inspired them to investigate and become active in the environmental movement. This, to me, is the single most significant factor that keeps me motivated to continue to paint these giant works of art. I've said it many times: in order to save the whales, we must first appreciate how large, how beautiful and how intelligent they are. With the vehicle of public art, I hope to communicate the unique spirits these marine mammals possess. Painting them in their true life-size, I hope to communicate this on a grand scale and impact people in a way only the great whales could.

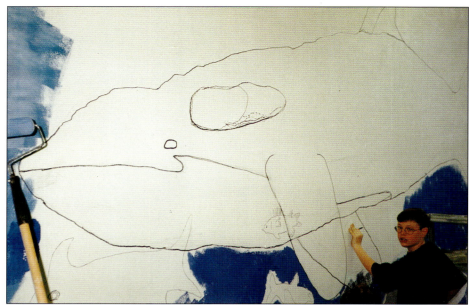
Point School mural project

Kids painting orca whale

Keepers of a clean healthy ocean

Finished school mural

March 24, 1994

Dear Wyland:

I am an elementary art teacher at Point School in St. Louis, Missouri. I had the opportunity to visit your Maui Gallery in June and purchased a print and a T-shirt. My sister visited the Maui Gallery upon my recommendation, and she purchased your wonderful book for me.

In January I took the book to one of my sixth grade rooms for their art history lesson. The students were so excited that we decided to make our own Whaling Wall in a stairwell near the classroom. The students helped draw on the wall with markers. Four boys were chosen to work as a group on the whale. The rest drew one fish or underwater details such as plant-life and coral. The next four classes (one hour each) we painted on the wall. The students were very creative in the way they worked around the height problem with the stairs. Often they would tape brushes or rollers to one or two yard sticks for the height. The last day our district painter let us borrow his extension pole to finish the water above the whale.

The entire school has enjoyed watching our whaling wall come to life. It has been a learning experience for all. The students have a new love for whales as well as your art work.

It would be the icing on a wonderful cake if you could respond to this letter in some way. Even though these sixth graders have never seen a Wyland Gallery or a Whaling Wall in real life, they have truly enjoyed reading about the life of an artist and viewing the pictures in the book. I have enclosed pictures (numbered on the back) for your enjoyment.

Thank you so much for your time. We anxiously await your response.

Sincerely
Peggy Dunsworth

Synchronicity, first in a series of 100 life-size fountain sculptures

Extinction of a whaling wall, Honolulu, HI

Teaching kids about whales

Young artists

Humpback whale airplane

Painting, dawn to dusk

Receiving Genesis Award, Loreta Switt - Discovery Television

WYLAND FOUNDATION VISION

The Wyland Foundation vision is to promote, respect and protect our precious ocean resources through life-size public art, education and awareness.

Currently one of the largest art projects in the world, the Whaling Walls, painted by America's Leading Environmental Marine Life Artist, Wyland, number over 67. The Wyland foundation will support his effort to complete 100 life-size murals by the year 2011.

The Wyland Foundation will also help fund a series of life-size bronze sculpture featuring endangered marine life in public places. Great whales, dolphins, manatees, sharks and other ocean creatures will be sculpted by Wyland and cast in bronze. The life-size sculpture will be featured in public places to be viewed by millions of people who may never have an opportunity to observe them in their natural habitat. Wyland's art is the next best thing to seeing the living creatures.

The Wyland Foundation will support a series of life-size fiberglass sculpture models to tour the world's art and natural history museums to teach and inspire people about the size and beauty of these unique animals.

We will continue to support other important environmental groups, individuals and programs locally, regionally and nationally.

We will continue to inspire, support and offer Wyland Foundation scholarships to gifted and needy child artists and naturalists.

The future of our planet is in the hands of our children. If we can inspire them through Wyland's art to learn more about protecting our natural resources, then it is worth all of our efforts.

Art has had a great impact on humankind since our beginning. Wyland's art has the unique ability to transform all who view it to a greater awareness. Wyland's art cannot be measured in goods or service, but in changed human beings.

Our goal is to inspire as many people as possible to learn more about our oceans and to encourage people to get involved. One person can indeed make a difference.

Classroom at the whaling wall

THE WHALING WALLS
LOCATIONS

1981 **WHALING WALL I "GRAY WHALE AND CALF"**
LAGUNA BEACH, CA
140 FEET LONG X 26 FEET HIGH
DEDICATED JULY 9TH, 1981
BY MRS. JOHN WAYNE
REPAINTED 1986

1982 **WHALING WALL II "YOUNG GRAY WHALE"**
ORANGE COUNTY MARINE INSTITUTE,
DANA POINT, CA
45 FEET LONG X 10 FEET HIGH
DEDICATED MARCH 20TH, 1982
BY BILL TOOMEY, OLYMPIC DECATHLON CHAMPION

1984 **WHALING WALL III "SPYHOPPING"**
MARINELAND, RANCHO PALOS VERDES, CA
20 FEET LONG X 30 FEET HIGH
DEDICATED JUNE 27TH, 1984
BY CLEVELAND AMORY, FUND FOR ANIMALS

1984 **WHALING WALL IV "THE GRAY WHALE FAMILY"**
WHITEROCK, BRITISH COLUMBIA, CANADA
70 FEET LONG X 30 FEET HIGH
DEDICATED SEPTEMBER 29TH, 1984
BY GORDON HOGG, MAYOR OF WHITEROCK

1985 **WHALING WALL V "THE ORCAS OF PUGET SOUND"**
SEATTLE, WA
140 FEET LONG X 50 FEET HIGH
DEDICATED NOVEMBER 10TH, 1984
BY IVAR HAGLUND, SEATTLE PORT MANAGER

1985 **WHALING WALL VI "HAWAIIAN HUMPBACKS"**
HONOLULU, HI
300 FEET LONG X 20 STORIES HIGH (1/2 ACRE)
DEDICATED APRIL 21ST, 1985
BY RUSS FRANCIS, SAN FRANCISCO 49ERS

1985 **WHALING WALL VII "CALIFORNIA GRAY WHALES"**
DEL MAR, CA
100 FEET LONG X 16 FEET HIGH
DEDICATED JULY 6TH, 1985
BY GLENN FREY, EAGLES SINGER/SONGWRITER

1985 **WHALING WALL VIII "ORCAS"**
VANCOUVER, BRITISH COLUMBIA, CANADA
130 FEET LONG X 70 FEET HIGH
DEDICATED SEPTEMBER 10TH, 1985
BY MICHAEL HARCOURT, MAYOR OF VANCOUVER

1986 **WHALING WALL IX "FIRST VOYAGE"**
POLYNESIAN CULTURAL CENTER, OAHU, HI
130 FEET LONG X 14 FEET HIGH
DEDICATED FEBRUARY 4TH, 1986
BY JOHN HILLERMAN, ACTOR

1986 **WHALING WALL X "MANATEES"**
ORLANDO, FL
14 FEET LONG X 8 FEET HIGH
DEDICATED 1986
BY JIMMY BUFFET, SINGER/SONGWRITER

1986 **WHALING WALL XI "FIRST BORN"**
SEA WORLD, ORLANDO, FL
30 FEET LONG X 12 FEET HIGH
DEDICATED SEPTEMBER 26TH, 1986
BY BILL EVANS, WASHINGTON, D.C.

1987 **WHALING WALL XII "LAGUNA COAST"**
2171 LAGUNA CANYON RD.
LAGUNA BEACH, CA
20 FEET LONG X 24 FEET HIGH
DEDICATED FEBRUARY 2ND, 1987
BY DARLENE WYLAND - ARTIST'S MOM

1987 **WHALING WALL XIII "A-5 POD"**
VICTORIA, BRITISH COLUMBIA, CANADA
130 FEET LONG X 7 STORIES HIGH
DEDICATED JUNE 20TH, 1987
IN MEMORY OF ROBIN MORTON
DEDICATED BY ROBERT BATEMAN - ARTIST

1987 **WHALING WALL XIV "SPERM WHALES"**
FUNABASHI, JAPAN
140 FEET LONG X 18 FEET HIGH
DEDICATED OCTOBER 14TH, 1987
BY DR. GORO TOMENAGA,
PROFESSOR EMERITUS OF TOKYO
UNIVERSITY AND MR. ONO, PRESIDENT
OF THE TOKYO BAY FISHING COUNCIL

1988 **WHALING WALL XV
"DOLPHINS OFF MAKAPUU POINT"**
SEA LIFE PARK, OAHU, HI
24 FEET LONG X 30 FEET HIGH
DEDICATED BY HENRY KAPONO,
SINGER/SONGRWRITER

1989 **WHALING WALL XVI "ORCAS OFF POINT LOMA"**
THE PLUNGE, MISSION BEACH
SAN DIEGO, CA
140 FEET LONG X 40 FEET HIGH
DEDICATED JUNE 29TH, 1989
BY BOB GAULT, PRESIDENT OF SEA WORLD

1989 **WHALING WALL XVII "BOTTLENOSE DOLPHINS"**
OSAKA, JAPAN
20 FEET LONG X 30 FEET HIGH
DEDICATED AUGUST 27TH, 1989
BY MR. TOSHITA AND KENT FABULOUS
WALL WAS PAINTED FOR A 24 HOUR TELEVISED
TELETHON IN JAPAN

1989 **WHALING WALL XVIII
"SPERM WHALES OF THE MEDITERRANEAN"**
NICE, FRANCE
42 FEET LONG X 120 FEET HIGH
DEDICATED 1989 - FRENCH DIGNITARY

1989 **WHALING WALL XIX "FORBIDDEN REEF"**
SEA WORLD, SAN DIEGO, CA
90 FEET LONG X 14 FEET HIGH
DEDICATED JULY 9TH, 1990
BY MICHAEL PEAK - AUTHOR

1990 **WHALING WALL XX "GRAY WHALE MIGRATION"**
SEA WORLD, SAN DIEGO, CA
80 FEET LONG X 15 FEET HIGH
DEDICATED JULY 9TH, 1990
BY BOB GAULT, PRESIDENT OF SEA WORLD

1990 **WHALING WALL XXI "WASHINGTON ORCAS"**
TACOMA, WA
120 FEET LONG X 45 FEET HIGH
DEDICATED JULY, 1990
BY TACOMA MAYOR KAREN VIALLE

1990 **WHALING WALL XXII (CEILING)
"ORCA HEAVEN"**
YAMAGATA, JAPAN
145 FEET LONG X 45 FEET HIGH
DEDICATED 1990
BY MR. KAWADA, PRESIDENT SUN MARINA

1990 **WHALING WALL XXIII
"BUNDABERG HUMPBACK FAMILY"**
BUNDABERG, AUSTRALIA
125 FEET LONG X 95 FEET HIGH
DEDICATED SEPTEMBER 28TH, 1990
BY JOHN NIELSEN

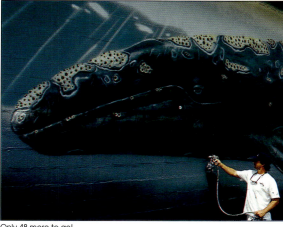

Only 48 more to go!

1990 **WHALING WALL XXIV
"HUMPBACK AND CALF"**
SYDNEY AQUARIUM, SYDNEY, AUSTRALIA
90 FEET LONG X 35 FEET HIGH
DEDICATED SEPTEMBER 28TH, 1990
BY JIM LONGLEY, PARLIAMENT NEW SOUTH WHALES

1990 **WHALING WALL XXV "HUMPBACKS"**
LAMPHERE HIGH SCHOOL, DETROIT, MI
110 FEET LONG X 15 FEET HIGH
DEDICATED OCTOBER 8TH, 1990
BY JAMES McCANN, SUPERINTENDENT -
LAMPHERE SCHOOL DISTRICT

1990 **WHALING WALL XXVI "SPERM WHALES AND
FLORIDA KEYS REEF"**
MARATHON KEYS, FL
150 FEET LONG X 20 FEET HIGH
DEDICATED OCTOBER 30TH, 1990
BY MARATHON KEYS FORMER MAYOR

1990 **WHALING WALL XXVII "MINKE WHALES"**
MUSEUM OF NATURAL HISTORY,
MARATHON KEYS, FL
40 FEET LONG X 8 FEET HIGH
DEDICATED OCTOBER 30TH, 1990
BY MANDY RODRIGUEZ, DOLPHIN RESEARCH CENTER

1991 **WHALING WALL XXVIII
"A TIME FOR CONSERVATION"**
KAUAI VILLAGE, KAUAI, HI
44 FEET HIGH WALL, 360 DEGREE MURAL
ON CLOCK TOWER
DEDICATED JANUARY 8TH, 1991
BY RON KOUCHI, COUNTY COUNCIL CHAIRMAN

1991 **WHALING WALL XXIX**
KAUAI , HI
150 FEET LONG X 24 FEET HIGH
DEDICATED JANUARY 8TH, 1991
BY PETER ALEVIZOS, KAUAI VILLAGE PRESIDENT

1991 **WHALING WALL XXX
"MAUI HUMPBACK BREACHING"**
LAHAINA, MAUI, HI
26 FEET LONG X 30 FEET HIGH
DEDICATED JANUARY 21ST, 1991
BY JOHN PITRE, SURREALIST ARTIST, AND JERRY
LOPEZ, RENOWNED SURFER

1991 **WHALING WALL XXXI
"GRAY WHALE MIGRATION"**
REDONDO BEACH, CA
586 FEET LONG X 100 FEET HIGH (1 1/4 ACRE)
DEDICATED JUNE 24TH, 1991
BY JOHN BRYSON, SOUTHERN CALIFORNIA EDISON

1991 **WHALING WALL XXXII "WHALES"**
TAIJI, JAPAN
30 FEET X 60 FEET
DEDICATED AUGUST, 1991
BY TAIJI TOWN MAYOR

1992 **WHALING WALL XXXIII "PLANET OCEAN"**
LONG BEACH, CA
1,280 FEET LONG X 105 FEET HIGH
DEDICATED JULY 9, 1992
BY CHRIS ROBINSON, ACTOR
**GUINNESS WORLD BOOK OF RECORDS
MAY 4, 1992**

1993 **WHALING WALL XXXIV
"OCEAN BIOSPHERE"**
BIOSPHERE 2
ORACLE, AZ
110 FEET LONG X 30 FEET HIGH
DEDICATED APRIL 18, 1993
BY LLOYD BRIDGES-ACTOR

1993 **WHALING WALL XXXV
"ORCAS OF THE OREGON COAST"**
FOX THEATER
PORTLAND, OR
120 FEET LONG X 60 FEET HIGH
DEDICATED MAY 9, 1993
BY DARLENE WYLAND - MOTHER'S DAY

THE WHALING WALLS
LOCATIONS

1993 WHALING WALL XXXVI
"WHALES OFF THE GULF OF MAINE"
BIW BUILDING - MAINE STATE PIER
PORTLAND, ME
1,000 FEET LONG X 25 FEET HIGH
DEDICATED JUNE 7, 1993
BY STEVEN KATONA, PRESIDENT OF THE
COLLEGE OF THE ATLANTIC AND MAYOR
ANNE PRINGLE

1993 WHALING WALL XXXVII
"ISLE OF SHOALS HUMPBACKS"
CABOT HOUSE - 64 VAUGHAN MALL
PORTSMOUTH, NH
220 FEET LONG X 40 FEET HIGH
DEDICATED JUNE 14, 1993 BY
MAYOR EILEEN FOLEY

1993 WHALING WALL XXXVIII
"STELLWAGON BANK HUMPBACKS"
33 TRAVELER ST.
BOSTON, MA
110 FEET LONG X 125 FEET HIGH
DEDICATED JUNE 21, 1993
BY JOHN WALSH
PRESIDENT OF W.S.P.A.

1993 WHALING WALL XXXIX
"FINBACK WHALES"
145 CRARY ST.
PROVIDENCE, RI
280 FEET LONG X 24 FEET HIGH
DEDICATED JUNE 28, 1993
BY MAYOR VINCENT CIANCI

1993 WHALING WALL XL
"INNER CITY WHALES"
41st. STREET UNDERPASS
NEW YORK, NY
460 FEET LONG X 22 FEET HIGH
DEDICATED JULY 5, 1993
BY JIM FOWLER, MUTUAL OMAHA'S
"WILD KINGDOM"

1993 WHALING WALL XLI
"THE GREAT SPERM WHALES"
124 CAPTAIN'S WALK & STATE ST.
NEW LONDON, CT
170 FEET LONG X 35 FEET HIGH
DEDICATED JULY 12, 1993
BY GOVERNOR LOWELL WEIKER

1993 WHALING WALL XLII
"EAST COAST HUMPBACKS"
2400 MARKET ST.
PHILADELPHIA, PA
125 FEET LONG X 130 FEET HIGH
DEDICATED JULY 19, 1993
BY MAYOR EDWARD RENDELL

1993 WHALING WALL XLIII
"HUMPBACKS OFF THE JERSEY COAST"
3800 BOARDWALK MALL
WILDWOOD, NJ
220 FEET LONG X 30 FEET HIGH
DEDICATED JULY 26, 1993
BY MAYOR EDMUND GRANT

1993 WHALING WALL XLIV
"DELAWARE MARINE MAMMALS"
117 MARKET ST.
WILMINGTON, DE
90 FEET LONG X 60 FEET HIGH
DEDICATED AUGUST 2, 1993
BY GOVERNOR TOM CARPER, MAYOR JIM SILLS &
SENATOR BILL ROTH

1993 WHALING WALL XLV
"DOLPHINS, SMALL-TOOTH MAMMALS"
3000 CONNECTICUT AVE. N.W.
WASHINGTON, D.C.
30 FEET LONG X 15 FEET HIGH
DEDICATED AUGUST 9, 1993
BY DR. ROGER PAYNE,
RENOWNED WHALE RESEARCHER

1993 WHALING WALL XLVI
"EXTINCT ATLANTIC GRAY WHALES"
600 W. HAMBURG ST.
BALTIMORE, MD
260 FEET LONG X 20 FEET HIGH
DEDICATED AUGUST 16, 1993
BY MAYOR KURT L. SCHMOKE

1993 WHALING WALL XLVII
"HUMPBACKS OFF VIRGINIA COAST"
999 WATERSIDE DR.
NORFOLK, VA
22,400 SQ. FT. - 280 FEET LONG X 80 FEET
DEDICATED AUGUST 23, 1993
BY MAYOR MASON ANDREWS
DEDICATED TO JACQUES COUSTEAU

1993 WHALING WALL XLVIII
"COASTAL DOLPHINS"
503 NUTT ST.
WILMINGTON, NC
40 FEET LONG X 30 FEET HIGH
DEDICATED AUGUST 30, 1993
BY MAYOR DON BETZ

1993 WHALING WALL XLIX
"RIGHT WHALES OFF THE CAROLINA COAST"
2101 N. OAK ST.
MYRTLE BEACH, SC
250 FEET LONG X 50 FEET HIGH
DEDICATED SEPTEMBER 6, 1993
BY MAYOR BOB GRISOM

1993 WHALING WALL L
"ATLANTA'S RIGHT WHALES"
90 CENTRAL AVE.
ATLANTA, GA
450 FEET LONG X 5 STORIES (50 FEET) HIGH
DEDICATED SEPTEMBER 13, 1993
BY MAYOR MAYNARD JACKSON

1993 WHALING WALL LI
"FLORIDA'S DOLPHINS"
1600 W. THOMPSON PKWY.
SARASOTA, FL
45 FEET LONG X 26 FEET HIGH
DEDICATED SEPTEMBER 20, 1993
BY MICHAEL MARTIN

1993 WHALING WALL LII
"FLORIDA'S LIVING REEF"
201 WILLIAMS ST.
KEY WEST, FL
52 FEET LONG X 45 FEET HIGH
DEDICATED SEPTEMBER 27, 1993
BY CAPTAIN TONY

1994 WHALING WALL LIII "ORCAS OFF THE GULF OF MEXICO"
SOUTH PADRE ISLAND CONV. CENTER
SOUTH PADRE ISLAND, TEXAS
265 FEET LONG X 25 FEET HIGH
DEDICATED MARCH 14, 1994

1994 WHALING WALL LIV
"ALASKA'S MARINE LIFE"
J.C. PENNEY
406 W. 5TH AVE.
ANCHORAGE, ALASKA
400 FEET LONG X 50 FEET HIGH
DEDICATED AUGUST 8, 1994
BY MAYOR RICK MYSTRON

1994 WHALING WALL LV "ORCAS A-30 SUBPOD"
VANCOUVER AQUARIUM
STANLEY PARK
VANCOUVER, BC, CANADA
175 FEET LONG X 14 FEET HIGH
DEDICATED AUGUST 15, 1994
BY DR. JOHN FORD IN MEMORY OF MIKE BIGG

1994 WHALING WALL LVI
"VANCOUVER ISLAND ORCAS"
OLD CONTINENTAL HOTEL
1290 GRANVILLE
VANCOUVER, BC, CANADA
DEDICATED AUGUST 15, 1994
BY DR. JOHN FORD

1994 WHALING WALL LVII "LEAP OF FAITH"
QUALITY INN
2224 EIGHTH AVE.
SEATTLE, WASHINGTON
30 FEET WIDE X 50 FEET HIGH
DEDICATED AUGUST 22, 1994
BY GOVERNOR MIKE LOWERY

1994 WHALING WALL LVIII
"ORCAS OFF THE SAN JUAN ISLANDS"
QUALITY INN
2224 EIGHTH AVE.
SEATTLE, WASHINGTON
30 FEET LONG X 50 FEET HIGH
DEDICATED AUGUST 22, 1994
BY MAYOR NORM RICE

1994 WHALING WALL LIX
"GRAY WHALES OFF THE OREGON COAST"
DEPOE BAY FISH COMPANY
617 SW BAY BLVD.
NEWPORT, OREGON
100 FEET LONG X 35 FEET HIGH
DEDICATED AUGUST 29, 1994
BY MAYOR MARK COLLSON AND DR. MATE

1994 WHALING WALL LX "SPYHOPPING GRAY WHALES"
PIER 39 - PARKING STRUCTURE ENTRANCE
BEACH AND EMBARCADERO
SAN FRANCISCO, CALIFORNIA
52 FEET LONG X 58 FEET HIGH
DEDICATED SEPTEMBER 5, 1994
BY DENNIS BOUEY

1994 WHALING WALL LXI
"GRAYS OFF SAN FRANCISCO COAST"
PIER 39 - AQUARIUM ENTRANCE
BEACH & EMBARCADERO
SAN FRANCISCO, CALIFORNIA
68 FEET LONG X 20 FEET HIGH
DEDICATED SEPTEMBER 5, 1994
BY MAYOR FRANK JORDAN

1994 WHALING WALL LXII "CELEBRATING GRAY WHALES"
MANN'S CHINESE THEATER
6901 HOLLYWOOD BOULEVARD
HOLLYWOOD, CALIFORNIA
152 FEET LONG X 37 FEET HIGH
DEDICATED SEPTEMBER 12, 1994
BY JOHNNY GRANT

1994 WHALING WALL LXIII "LIFE-SIZE BLUE WHALES"
PARAMOUNT PICTURES
5555 MELROSE AVE.
HOLLYWOOD, CALIFORNIA
180 FEET LONG X 85 FEET HIGH
DEDICATED, SEPTEMBER 12, 1994
BY EARL LESTZ, PRESIDENT OF PARAMOUNT

1994 WHALING WALL LXIV "SAN DIEGO MIGRATION"
SAN DIEGO NATIONAL BANK
1420 KETTNER BOULEVARD
SAN DIEGO, CALIFORNIA
160 FEET LONG X 60 FEET HIGH
DEDICATED, SEPTEMBER 19, 1994
BY MAYOR SUSAN GOLDING

1994 WHALING WALL LXV
"FRIENDLY GRAYS OFF SAN IGNACIO"
UNIVERSITY SCIENCE MUSEUM
MEXICO CITY, MEXICO
85 FEET LONG X 20 FEET HIGH
DEDICATED SEPTEMBER 26, 1994
BY DR. JORGE FLORES VALDES

1994 WHALING WALL LXVI "FREE KEIKO"
EL NUEVO REINO AVENTURA
AL AJUSCO 1500
MEXICO CITY, MEXICO
200 FEET LONG X 45 FEET HIGH
DEDICATED SEPTEMBER 26, 1994
BY ALEJANDRO AZCUE CARRILLO

1995 WHALING WALL LXVII "EARTH DAY HAWAII"
ROYAL ALOHA CONDOMINIUMS
1909 ALA WAI BLVD.
HONOLULU, HAWAII
40 FEET LONG X 160 FEET HIGH
DEDICATED APRIL 22, 1995
25TH ANNIVERSARY OF EARTH DAY
BY PAT MORITA, ACTOR

WYLAND ART AVAILABLE AT THESE FINE LOCATIONS AROUND THE WORLD:

CALIFORNIA

Wyland Studio Gallery
509 S. Coast Highway
Laguna Beach, CA 92651
1-800-WYLAND-1
714-376-8000
714-494-8357 Fax

Canyon Gallery
2171 Laguna Canyon Road
Laguna Beach, CA 92651
1-800-WYLAND-0
714-497-4081
714-497-7852 Fax

Laguna Beach - Downtown
218 Forest Ave.
Laguna Beach, CA 92651
1-800-995-6509
714-497-9494
714-497-2298 Fax

San Diego
855 W. Harbor Dr. Suite A.
San Diego, CA 92101
1-800-995-2635
619-544-9995
619-544-0945 Fax

San Francisco
Pier 39 - Suite M-209
San Francisco, CA 94133
1-800-889-9526
415-398-1922
415-398-4105 Fax

FLORIDA

Orlando
The Crossroads*
12541 State Rd. #535
Orlando, FL 32836
407-827-1110
407-827-1108 Fax

Lake Buena Vista
Disney's Boardwalk*
2101 N. Epcot Resorts Blvd.
Lake Buena Vista, FL 32830
407-560-8750
407-560-8752 Fax

Celebration*
681 Front Street, Suite 100
Celebration, FL 34747
407-566-1020
407-566-1022 Fax

Key West*
719 Duval St.
Key West, FL 33040
1-800-469-3069
305-292-9711
305-292-9669 Fax

Key West*
102 Duval St.
Key West, FL 33040
1-800-469-3069
305-294-5240
305-294-5250 Fax

Sarasota*
465 John Ringling Blvd.
St. Armands Circle
Sarasota, FL 34236
941-388-5331
941-388-5234

Sanibel*
703 Tarpon Bay Road, Suite B-C
Sanibel, FL 33957
941-472-3366
941-472-3327 Fax

Naples*
1814 9th St. North
Naples, FL 34102
941-649-3232
941-649-6776 Fax

Destin
Paradise Galleries*
151 Calhoun Ave. #606
Destin, FL 32541
904-650-0890

ALASKA

Ketchikan
Northern Visions Gallery*
76 Front Street
Ketchikan, AK 99901
907-225-2858
907-247-2856 Fax

OREGON

Portland
711 SW 10th Ave.
Portland, OR 97205
1-800-578-7316
503-223-7692
503-223-7692 Fax

NEVADA

Las Vegas*
Fashion Show Mall
3200 S. Las Vegas. Suite 322
Las Vegas, NV 89109
702-699-9970
702-699-9965 Fax

ARIZONA

Scottsdale
Desert Oceans*
4223 N. Marshal Way, Suite 2
Scottsdale, AZ 85251
602-423-3535
602-423-3534 Fax

MINNESOTA

Bloomington
Ocean Encounters*
Mall of America - 208 South Avenue
Bloomington, MN 55425
612-853-0191
612-853-0184 Fax

WISCONSIN

Madison
Nature's Gallery*
6712 Odana Road
Madison, WI 53719
608-827-5841
608-827-5844 Fax

NEW YORK

South Hampton
Chrysalis Gallery*
92 Main Street
South Hampton, NY 11968
516-287-1887
516-287-1884 Fax

NEW JERSEY

Avalon
Sea Life Galleries*
2900 Dune Drive
Avalon, NJ 08202
609-368-7300
609-368-6760 Fax

SOUTH CAROLINA

Hilton Head Island
Endangered Arts*
South Island Square, Unit B
Hilton Head Island, SC 29928
803-785-7205

TEXAS

San Antonio
Wyland Galleries of Texas*
349 E. Commerce St., Suite 303
San Antonio, TX 78205
1-800-WYLAND-6
210-472-1266

HAWAII

OAHU

Haleiwa Gallery
66-150 Kamehameha Hwy.
Haleiwa, HI 96712
808-637-7498
808-637-5469 Fax

Waikiki Gallery
Hyatt Regency Waikiki
2424 Kalakaua Ave.
Honolulu, HI 96815
808-924-3133
808-924-3622 Fax

Waikiki Gallery II
Wyland Kalakaua Center
2155 Kalakaua Ave. #104
Honolulu, HI 96815
808-924-1322
808-924-3518 Fax

Aloha Tower Marketplace
101 Ala Moana Blvd. Sp. 191, 7B
Honolulu. HI 96813
808-536-8973
808-536-8981 Fax

MAUI

Lahaina
136 Dickenson St.
Lahaina, HI 96761
808-661-0590
808-661-4467 Fax

Lahaina II
711 Front Street
Lahaina, HI 96761
808-667-2285
808-661-4511 Fax

Lahaina III
697 Front Street
Lahaina, HI 96761
808-661-7099
808-661-4750 Fax

BIG ISLAND

Hilton Waikaloa Village
Waikaloa Beach Resort
Waikaloa, HI 96734
808-885-5258
808-885-5384 Fax

Waterfront Row
75-5770 Alii Drive
Kailua-Kona, HI 96740
808-334-0037
808-329-5398 Fax

King's Shop Waikaloa
69-250 Waikaloa Beach Drive
Waikaloa, HI 96743
808-885-8882
808-885-7219 Fax

KAUAI

Kauai Village
4-831 Kuhio Highway
Kapaa, HI 96746
808-822-9855
808-822-4156 Fax

Poipu Shopping Village
2360 Kiahuna Plantation Drive
Koloa, HI 96756
808-742-6030
808-742-4739 Fax

*Distributorship